THE GREEN LINE

HOLIDAY IN A WARZONE
CYPRUS 1974

Soner Kioufi

*To Deirdre
Hope you enjoy my book!
Best Wishes*

eyyaPublishing

13-3-13

THE GREEN LINE
HOLIDAY IN A WARZONE
- CYPRUS 1974 -

All Rights Reserved

No part of this book may be reproduced in any form, by photocopying or by any electronic or mechanical means, including information storage or retrieval systems, without permission in writing from both the copyright owner and the publisher of this book.

ISBN: 978-0-9571739-6-5

First Published 28-02-2012
by
EYYA Publishing
4 Oakfield Road
Croydon
CR0 2UA
United Kingdom

Cover by Ceylan Kioufi
Edited by Patrick Morgan

Web site by eyya Web Design
www.eyya.com

Printed in Great Britain by eyyaPrint
www.eyyaprint.com

ACKNOWLEDGMENTS

While travelling on the journey of life you inevitably meet some extraordinary people along the way, and some of those I've met have inspired me to write this book. I wish to express my deep gratitude to them.

First, my mother Munevver and father Hassan, who were among the first generation to leave the shores of Cyprus to establish a home in England. They worked so hard to provide the best possible start in life for their children, in a country that offered great opportunities regardless of financial status.

My brothers and sisters – Ilker, Mehmet, Hicran, Feriha, Ayse, Niazy and Erden – have also made this story possible while supporting each other in early life, through thick and thin.

I would like to thank, for their support while I was writing this book, my daughter Ceylan (who designed the cover) and my wife Po Kam; and friends Peggie Dunne, David Boost and Francisco De Souza, without whose encouragement I might not have completed the process. Long time friend, Maria (Georgiou) Christophi, for offering her time to proof read. My thanks also go to Eleni Kyriacou for her invaluable feedback and advice on the structure and content of the story.

Finally, a very big thank you to Patrick Morgan, who has spent a lot of time researching and editing, giving my story a good chance of actually being published.

*"I'm Greek Cypriot.
Soner is not, that is apparent in this book.
He's my friend and I've known him since we were at college together but nothing prepared me for this book. The memories he now shares with you are ones that even I have never been privy to.*

It's an honest book, neither hyped nor unapologetic, and is a must read for both Greek Cypriots and Turkish Cypriots of our generation.

*Cry.... With laughter you will.....
Parts will shock you...*

He conjures up some images we, from the island are all familiar with......some, thankfully not....."

Maria (Georgiou) Christophi

CONTENTS

    Prologue 1
1. We're all going on a summer holiday 8
2. A South London childhood 14
3. Turkish Cypriots immigrate to the UK 30
4. A step back in time 38
5. Cyprus life 46
6. Samson in power 52
7. History before my eyes 60
8. Turkey intervenes 71
9. Trench warfare 81
10. What is it like to be dead? 97
11. Pure torture 118
12. Thoughts of home 124
13. Visiting a mysterious friend 133
14. Return home to another war 142
    Epilogue 146

PROLOGUE

One day in 1964, Major-General Peter Young, the British Army officer in charge of the operations of an international peace force in Cyprus, took an old dark green chinagraph pencil, thought for a moment and then drew a line on a map of Nicosia, the capital city. He had just created what would become known the world over as the Green Line, and he had also effectively divided an island in two.

Young's pencil mark defined a ceasefire line that separated the Greek and Turkish communities of Cyprus as the island experienced a post-independence period of strife. It was to take on greater significance in 1974 when, tensions on the island having continued for a further decade, Greek interests attempted a coup d'état, Nikos Sampson was installed as president and Turkish armed forces found themselves forced to intervene to protect their Turkish Cypriot compatriots. The Green Line had been extended.

The Green Line marks the southernmost point to which the occupying Turkish forces advanced in 1974, when the events related in this book took place. It now forms the border between the Greek Republic of Cyprus in the south of the island and the Turkish Republic of Northern Cyprus. Across the island, for more than a hundred and eighty kilometres, now runs the United Nations Buffer Zone, which follows the line of Young's 1964 pencil mark and which is the responsibility of the successor to his peace force, the United Nations Peacekeeping Force in Cyprus.

* * * * *

Man has inhabited Cyprus since the Stone Age, but the Bronze Age brought increased trade with the outside world as well as settlement over the centuries by Greeks, Phoenicians, Egyptians and Persians among others. A period of rule by Alexander the Great was followed by a time of Greek influence then, in 58 BCE, rule by the Romans. When their Empire was divided in two, Cyprus became part of the Eastern Roman Empire, otherwise known as Byzantium, with Constantinople at its centre.

The island's Byzantine period was ended in the twelfth century AD by Richard the Lionheart, who took possession of the island and promptly sold it to the Knights Templar. The Templars, in turn, sold it to the Poitevin crusader Guy de Lusignan in 1192. Cyprus was ruled under the feudal system, with the Catholic church officially replacing the Greek Orthodox, until 1489, when it was ceded to Venice.

The Venetians fortified the island against the Ottoman Empire but the preparations proved in vain, for in 1571 Cyprus fell to the Ottomans. And it remained part of the Ottoman Empire until 1878.

The British first took control of government in the island in 1878, when they reached a secret agreement – the Cyprus Convention – with the Ottoman Empire. In return, Britain agreed to support the Ottomans' Sultan at that year's Congress of Berlin, whose aim was to reorganise the countries of the Balkans to the satisfaction of all parties. Despite the apparent initial success of the Congress, its long-term effect was to prove disastrous. Resentment over the allocation of territories festered for many years and helped to lead, eventually, to the outbreak of world war in 1914.

In assuming control of Cyprus, Britain also agreed to safeguard the presence of a Muslim religious tribunal, Muslim schools and other religious establishments on the island.

Three years after taking over, the British carried out a census in the new protectorate, which found that, of the island's population of 186,000, just under three-quarters were Greek and nearly a quarter were Turkish.

There was some initial optimism about the future of the country, but the honeymoon period didn't last long; the Cypriot people were forced to pay heavy taxes to the British administration for which they received little in return. In addition, there was tension between the Greek and Turkish communities, while Greeks began to explore the idea of union with their mother country and Turks advocated the partition of the island.

In 1914, with the start of the first world war and the Ottoman Empire lining up against Britain and its partners, the situation changed dramatically, and the UK annexed Cyprus. Things changed again when the island was declared a Crown Colony in 1925.

Greek Cypriots' demands for enosis (union with Greece) grew louder amid British attempts to silence the protests, which continued after the second world war under the leadership of the charismatic Archbishop Makarios, head of the Cypriot Orthodox Church. Finally, violence ensued as EOKA, the Greek National Organisation of Cypriot Fighters, attacked British targets.

Simultaneous attacks on targets in Nicosia and Famagusta on 1 April 1955 brought the attention of the world to EOKA's campaign, which was aimed at ridding Cyprus of the 'British yoke' and achieving the longed-for union with Greece. EOKA's military leader, George Grivas, had plenty of experience to call on: he had fought for Greece in both world wars and in the Greek civil war of the 1940s.

At first, EOKA's targets were primarily British, but it wasn't long before Turkish Cypriots – particularly those supporting British security forces – came under fire.

British colonial policies also promoted ethnic polarisation. The British applied the principle of 'divide and rule', setting the two groups against each other to prevent combined action against colonial rule. For example, when Greek Cypriots rebelled in the 1950s, the colonial administration established an all-Turkish police force, known as the Auxiliary Police, to combat them. This and similar practices contributed to inter-communal animosity.

The Green Line

It is estimated that in 1958, EOKA killed fifty-five Turkish Cypriots while the Turkish resistance (TMT) organisation's toll of Greeks was sixty.

Finally, in 1960, Cyprus gained independence from Britain, with both enosis and partition prohibited under the agreement, a president (Archbishop Makarios III) elected by the Greek community and a vice-president (Dr Fazıl Küçük) chosen by the Turkish Cypriot population.

The first Turkish intervention in Cyprus occurred on 20 July 1974, when troops landed on the northern coast, at Kyrenia. The action, said Turkey, was intended to ensure the safety of Turkish Cypriots and guarantee the country's independence in the aftermath of the coup that had deposed Makarios and installed Nikos Sampson as president.

Turkey's forces were met by resistance from Greeks and Greek Cypriots. A ceasefire was agreed three days later, by which time the Turkish forces had secured a narrow corridor between Kyrenia and Nicosia.

On 23 July 1974, the ruling junta in Greece collapsed, chiefly as a result of the events in Cyprus, and Sampson renounced the presidency. Peace talks aimed at resolving the Cyprus problem started in Geneva on July 25.

Turkish forces launched the second phase of their intervention on 14 August 1974, quickly occupying around a third of the island. The operation resulted in thousands of Greek Cypriots becoming refugees and many prisoners being taken.

Cyprus has continued to have its share of troubles since the events of 1974.

In 1983, the Turkish Republic of Northern Cyprus was proclaimed by Turkish Cypriots, and it has continued to exist despite only being recognised by Turkey. Sporadic attempts to resolve the Cyprus problem have failed, although hopes that the island can resume its once harmonious existence have never disappeared.

* * * * *

After Sicily and Sardinia, Cyprus is the third largest of the islands in the Mediterranean, and the biggest in the eastern sector of that sea. Measuring two hundred and forty kilometres from west to east and a hundred from north to south, it sits seventy-five kilometres from the nearest point in Turkey and eight hundred from the Greek mainland.

From the north of the island you can make out the outline of the Taurus Mountains in Turkey, and there are matching mountainous areas in Cyprus: the Troodos and Kyrenia ranges, which encircle the central Mesaoria plain. Lower-lying land stretches to the coasts.

Nowadays, Cyprus has four distinct areas: the Turkish Republic of Northern Cyprus occupies the upper third of the island, while the Republic of Cyprus accounts for the rest, apart from a United Nations-controlled buffer zone between the two territories and the two British-controlled bases of Akrotiri and Dhekelia.

Despite its troubles, Cyprus has for centuries been known as an island paradise, bathed by the warm waters of the Mediterranean and attracting hordes of visitors seeking leisure, refuge, wealth or peace. Holidaymakers in their millions are still drawn to its beaches, its silent villages and its throbbing resorts.

In the summer of 1974, members of one south London family flew to Cyprus to begin what they hoped would be a holiday they would never forget. Their wishes were granted.

CHAPTER ONE

We're all going on a summer holiday

Thump! The dry Mediterranean heat introduced itself with a body blow as I climbed down from the Boeing 747. I'd never before experienced such temperatures; then again, I was only eight and my horizons up to that point had been limited to south London's dull, grey skies. I knew little of the world beyond Tooting or what it had to offer.

The year was 1974, the place was Nicosia Airport in Cyprus and the experiences that were to follow will be branded in my brain for as long as I live.

* * * * *

My name is Soner Kioufi, or Küfi to those blessed with a smattering of the Turkish language. I'm the son of Turks from Cyprus – or Kıbrıs, if you prefer to give the island its Turkish name. My father, Hassan Küfi, was a Turkish Cypriot who, like many of his compatriots, fought with the British army in the Second World War. Captured by the Germans, he spent the last five years of the conflict as a prisoner of war.

Dad was born in a small village called Kritou Tera, and had two older sisters. He came from a strict Muslim background; as a child he was fascinated by the violin but his mother wouldn't allow him to take lessons because the violin bow, when placed over the strings, formed a cross: a symbol of Christianity.

Dad, in turn, became quite strict – he needed only to raise his voice for us kids to be shaking in our boots – but he never laid a finger on us.

Clean cut and with a big frame, he stood around five feet seven tall and had brown eyes and short grey hair that was always combed back. Dad, who was 54 when I was born, always wore a shirt and tie, smart trousers and polished shoes. He would never let us buy jeans and he hated modern music with a passion, blaming the Beatles for bringing the object of his hatred to the UK.

"What is this danga-dungu-danga-dungu, yeah-yeah-yeah-yeah-yeah?" he would demand in Turkish. "Turn that rubbish off!" Then he would play some old–time Turkish ballad or other, insisting: "Listen, this is what you call music and singing – not shouting and banging."

Dad nurtured a similar hatred for men sporting the long hair that was fashionable at the time in the 60s and 70s. Every male under his roof, therefore, had to have very, very short hair – cut by Dad himself. When we were little he would use scissors but he later bought a Bressant manual hair clipper. Once the blades had become blunt through vigorous use, it was off to the barbershop, with 'short back and sides' the usual request on our monthly visit.

After three weeks he would look at our slowly lengthening hair, rub his chin and say: "Looks like we need to make another visit to the barber soon." The following week we would all be off to see his Greek Cypriot friend Theo, the barber in Balham, whose shop had the traditional striped pole outside.

We would spend at least an hour there while Theo cut my two younger brothers' hair, then mine and last my dad's. All the while, Dad would be speaking in Greek to Theo about the two subjects he was passionate about: politics and history.

Dad got on famously with both the Greek and Turkish communities in London, and everyone respected him and enjoyed his company. He loved to laugh and to make people laugh, and wherever we went you could guarantee the room would be filled with merriment sooner or later.

I remember Dad telling me stories he found so funny that he couldn't get the words out. The tears would be running down his cheeks, and you couldn't help but join in because his laughter was so contagious. It didn't matter that he couldn't get to the end of the story.

Yes, Dad could be tough and stubborn, yet his softer side was on show most of the time.

* * * * *

Turks in Cyprus didn't use surnames; instead, they were given a name at birth that was followed by their father's first name.

The Green Line

My dad's given name was Hassan and his father's first name was Küfi, so Dad was called Hassan Küfi.

As well as Turkish and Greek, Dad was also fluent in German and adapted to the English language. The few years he spent at school had taught him the old Ottoman Turkish writing, which used Arabic script, but he didn't understand the Roman characters that have been in use since Mustafa Kemal Atatürk, the Republic of Turkey's first president, introduced them in 1928. Imagine, even the most educated Turks had suddenly become illiterate overnight.

Under the British colonial rule of Cyprus he had been asked his name and British officials had written it down for him. And that's where the spelling Kioufi came from: it's a very precise spelling of my father's pronunciation of the Turkish name Küfi.

In the late 1950s, he left Cyprus and emigrated to the UK, leaving his wife and son behind on the tense, troubled island. Once he had settled in London, he sent tickets enabling his wife and son to join him. Sadly though, his wife found herself unable to adapt to the new environment of England and returned to Cyprus, taking their son, Üner, with her.

In the years that followed, Hassan met my mother, who had left a violent relationship as a result of which five children had already been born. I followed, in 1965. My father wanted to follow custom by naming me after his father, but answering to the name of Kioufi Kioufi (or Küfi Küfi) would have been distinctly odd. So it was that my mother came to name me Soner, and everyone in the family just called me Küfi.

Mum was much younger than Dad – 28 years younger, to be precise. She would have been only 24 and he around 52 when they met.

Mum, rather short and somewhat overweight, was fair-skinned and had blue eyes and brown hair. At times a tough character – she was not afraid to say what was on her mind if someone upset her – she nevertheless showed a sensitive and shy side until she got to know someone.

She loved her jewellery and make-up, and kept up with the times when it came to fashion: in the 50s the beehive hairdo, the girdle and swing dress; in the 60s the Mary Quant mini skirt and bouffant hairstyle. Mum loved her Turkish books and read romantic novels whenever there was a spare moment. She also enjoyed the new musical sounds of the 60s and 70s.

Brought up in traditional Cypriot village life, Mum looked after her three youngest brothers, cooked and cleaned and did as she was told; there was no time for idleness. She came from a family of seven – two older sisters and four younger brothers – who lived with their parents in a small house in Lefkoniko, now in the Turkish sector of the island.

At the age of fifteen, she was sent to England to get married – a marriage that had been arranged by her parents.

* * * * *

The Green Line

What an extraordinary feeling; stepping off the aircraft stairs on to the scorching Nicosia ground, it felt as if the rubber soles of my shoes were at melting point. I was used to the more temperate climes of my London home and nothing had prepared me for these temperatures.

But what a great time I was going to have on this yearned-for holiday, my first ever. Already, its first, weird experiences had filled me with delight. I had been so excited about the trip that I had been practising Cliff Richard's 60s hit *Summer Holiday* for weeks, and daydreaming about bursting into song on the plane, with all the passengers joining in.

We're going where the sun shines brightly.
We're going where the sea is blue.
We've seen it in the movies,
Now let's see if it's true.

Naturally, it didn't turn out that way, for I was a shy boy and didn't have the nerve to sing out loud to a cabin full of bemused strangers. Instead, I contented myself with singing the song in my head and smiling all the way to Cyprus.

CHAPTER TWO

A South London childhood

My parents ran a fish and chip shop in Tooting, South London. The task of looking after me and my two younger brothers, Niazy and Erden, fell to our older half-brothers, İlker and Mehmet, and half-sisters, Hicran (pronounced Hijran), Feriha (Feri for short) and Ayşe (pronounced Ayesha).

In the early 1970s, ours was a council house full of noise: from us kids, from our old black and white TV, from songs blaring out from the radio or from the record player, which played antiquated 78s as well as the newer 45s and 33s. When Mum was at home and Dad not around she would turn the volume up high every time *It Must Be Him*, by Vikki Carr, came on the radio, singing along to the chorus in her broken English:

Let it please be him, oh dear God,
It must be him , it must be him
or I shall die, Or – I – shall – die.

Ours was a house full of kids with dual personalities: when our parents were around we were quiet, obedient and respectful Turkish children; when we were home alone, we were wild and unruly London street kids. We spent most of our time out on the street, skipping or playing Had, Knock Down Ginger, Marbles, Knockers and Jax. During the time we lived at Balham's Kenilford Road, in the early 70s, we were the street's wild kids – and don't forget, there were eight of us.

The two older brothers, İlker and Mehmet, took part in a never-ending, no-holds-barred battle for supremacy, fighting constantly, dealing out a ceaseless flow of punches and kicks.

Most of the time, when he found the time to stop scrapping, İlker, who was tall and thin, blue-eyed with thick, short, dark, fuzzy hair, would be working as an apprentice cinema projectionist. Otherwise, he would be studiously covering his adolescent face with a thick brown medicinal compound to treat his appallingly bad acne. The rest of his life was spent in hiding and cooking bacon behind my father's back.

Dad was a strict Muslim (although I have to say he liked his whisky and never went to the mosque), so any foodstuff made from the 'flesh of swine' and prohibited by the Qur'an was forbidden in our house. So every time İlker cooked his beloved bacon while our parents were out, we all knew we were in for a row. My sisters would always grass İlker up to Dad, and there would follow an almighty shouting and banging on İlker's locked bedroom door.

This was a scene that occurred with distressing regularity in our household.

One day, in the middle of a typical battle between İlker and Mehmet, Mehmet climbed up and through the skylight on to the roof in order to get away from his brother. My frantic sisters, scared out of their wits by his recklessness, were shouting from the street, imploring Mehmet to get down, but he just smiled in reply. İlker couldn't get him up here, he grinned; he was too much of a chicken to get out on to the roof.

"Who's the king now?" crowed Mehmet, sitting on his lofty perch and laughing fit to bust while the concerned neighbours called out the fire brigade to deal with the emergency.

"Who's the king?" was a question that my elder brothers posed constantly in our home. The 'king' was the undisputed boss of the household and each one of us kids had to bow down before him or suffer the painful consequences.

First the victim would be gripped fiercely in a neckhold and then would come the question: "who's the king?" If you were able to scream you would, but the longer you gasped for breath and withheld the answer, the tighter the hold would become. The key to gaining freedom from the hold lay in the magic words, "You're the king! You're the king!" Before he relaxed his grip, the 'king' might even administer one final, cruel squeeze to force the magic words out of you a third time.

The Green Line

All of us experienced the dreaded neck-hold at one time or another and, believe you me, you knew beyond all shadow of a doubt when you were about to gasp your last breath. We kids had no choice but to submit and declare the holder king; missing the chance may well have cost you your life. Once I thought I would box clever and submit as soon as the neck-hold was applied. Sadly, my ruse didn't work and I was made to endure the entire ordeal – and sound convincing as I finally submitted, into the bargain.

Mehmet, although the short one in the family, with straight, fine, light brown hair, darker complexion and blue eyes, was the good-looking one of the family – to himself if no one else. When he wasn't fighting or sitting on the roof, he could be found in front of a mirror, admiring what he perceived to be his good looks. But one day his vanity was turned upside down.

My oldest sister, Hicran, turned on the gas oven so she could cook dinner but, try as she might, she just couldn't get the gas to light. The way she held the matches upright meant they burned out before she could apply them to the gas source at the back of the oven. Enter Mehmet, who had heard Feri yelling at Hicran to be careful.

"What's the matter?" he demanded, as the seeping gas built up silently in the oven.

"She can't light the oven," replied Feri.

"Give the matches to the king, I'll show you how it's done, stupid," exclaimed Mehmet, grabbing the matchbox out of Hicran's hands. A thought occurred to him. "Did you turn the gas off?" he demanded.

"Yes", replied Hicran, "I'm not stupid, you know!"

Sinking to his knees, Mehmet stuck his head and shoulders into the oven and struck a match, with the inevitable explosive consequences.

"My face! My face!" screamed the horror-stricken Mehmet, with all those hours spent in front of the mirror flashing before his eyes. "You left the bloody gas on all this time, stupid cow!"

"Oh, I thought I'd turned it off," Hicran replied calmly.

Hicran, with shoulder-length, thick, dark brown hair and blue eyes, was always thought of as the dipsy one of the family. She spoke in soft tones, with almost everything that came out of her mouth ending up with a question.

She might have been an indecisive person but she was the one to go to if you had a problem as a kid. She would comfort you, try to find the root of the problem then try to deal with it. Of the eight kids in our family, she was the one with the biggest heart of gold, and she never showed a hint of selfishness.

As Feri was running out of the house screaming for help, Hicran was showing her natural calmness. Soon enough an ambulance arrived, siren screaming. Mehmet was ferried off to hospital, from where he later returned with his precious head and face wrapped in bandages, just like the Invisible Man.

My parents had always stressed how dangerous gas could be, and now we all knew how right they were. "I'm not lighting it, you light it," was the oft-heard refrain in the kitchen after that incident. I even remember Hicran arguing with Feri as to who should light the gas, then turning to me to do it for her. I was only about six years old and she would have been twelve at the time.

I can only guess at how anxious the vain Mehmet was as he removed the bandages a few days later. On our return from school, Feri stopped my younger brothers and me in the hallway.

"Mehmet has taken his bandages off and he's in the dining room. Just don't be scared when you see him, OK?" she pleaded.

Apprehensively, we walked into the dining room to find Mehmet facing away from us. He turned round suddenly and we stood transfixed in utter shock, mumbling words of revulsion. He had been transformed from the Invisible Man into Thing out of The Fantastic Four, his face covered in thick crusty scabs.

"You look ugly!" were the only words that came to my quivering lips.

Mehmet's response was to give me a stinging slap round the head. "When the scabs come off I'll still be the best-looking one in the house," he proclaimed, his pride in his appearance apparently unaffected by the experience. "Anyway, let this teach you all a lesson: never play with gas or matches!"

Out on the street, our favourite game, and an endless source of amusement, was Knock Down Ginger. Like anyone our age, we found it hilarious to watch people open their front doors only to find nobody there. We would watch from a distance, hidden behind a wall or car and stifling our sniggers until it was safe to laugh out loud, when the puzzled victims had shut their doors.

Once, Ayşe, youngest brother Erden and I ventured out to a newly built housing estate. Ayşe pointed out a door. "Küfi, you ring that doorbell and then run fast," she instructed. Was I one to turn down that kind of challenge? Not I.

Boldly, we walked up to the door, Ayşe nudged me and I rang the bell – but we stood stunned when the door opened with my hand still poised in the air. We'd never been caught before. How on earth were we going to get out of this one without a clout round the ear?

"Yes?" enquired the old gentleman who opened the door.

Ayşe was thinking fast. "Sorry, sir," she blurted out. "We've been followed by this weird-looking man and we're scared. Can we come in and call the police, please?" she improvised, a frightened look on her face.

Wow, she was good, really good. Her hastily plotted ruse had the potential to rescue us from being reported to our parents.

The best in the family at telling 'porky pies', Ayşe was quick-witted, convincing and very, very persuasive - she had all the makings of someone who would excel in estate agency or even law. The chubby one of the girls, she had thick, wavy, shoulder-length hair and brown eyes.

"Come in, come in," our 'victim' replied. "I've been watching you from my window and I sensed there was something wrong."

I was a little hesitant about entering the house, but I was nudged onwards by Ayşe. "We'll be safe here, come on," she urged.

I judged our host, whose face was cherry blossom pink and contrasted with short-cropped hair as white as snow, to be in his early sixties. His wife, sitting in the living room, was asking anxiously what the matter was as he followed us into the room. Their house was really nice, freshly decorated with new carpets and filled with desirable furniture. This was a palace compared to our humble home.

There was a large TV in the living room and, I noted with fascination, it was in colour. I had never known that colour televisions existed, let alone seen one, and I couldn't take my eyes off the man on the screen reading the news. Puzzled, I just could not understand how they made the picture in colour without going over the edges. My young, naive mind was comparing the TV to a colouring book and recalling how difficult it was to colour in without accidentally going over the black lines that outlined the picture.

In our home, there was only a black and white TV, which we had to feed with 50p pieces. We had to budget carefully and work out which programmes we wanted to watch as the box had the frustrating habit of cutting out mid-programme when our 50p had been used up. But my resourceful elder brothers worked out how to pick the lock on the TV with a penknife, take a few coins out of the box and feed them back in again, and it was not long before men from the TV company came and took the set away. My parents, too busy trying to earn enough to clothe and feed eight kids, didn't know what was going on until it was too late.

I managed to drag my attention away from the colour TV for a moment. "What did the man look like?" the old lady was asking.

"He was tall, with dark hair and a beard," replied Ayşe, without a second's hesitation.

Meanwhile, the man was dialling 999 on the black telephone that sat on a small side table. He explained everything clearly to the police and was told that officers would be at his house within minutes. I'm pretty sure I gulped at that point. I'm absolutely certain the thought "Oh my God! How are we going to get out of this?" was racing through my brain.

"The police will come down to take a statement from you, and they'll try to find this fellow," said the helpful man. A couple of minutes earlier we'd been hoping to get a good laugh out of him. Laughter was now the last thing on our minds.

"OK, I hope they find him," returned my sister. "He really did scare us, you know."

We all waited, sitting on the respectable couple's comfortable sofa. For me the tension was unbearable, but it was broken after about ten minutes by Ayşe getting to her feet.

"What's taking them so long?" she exclaimed. "I think we'd better get back home or our parents will be worried."

"Wait a little bit longer, they'll be here soon," urged the old lady.

"What do you think, Küfi?" Ayşe appealed to me.

"Yeah, Mum's gonna be really worried if we don't go now," I confirmed, twigging on to Ayşe's plan.

"Where do you live?" asked the old man. "I'll give the police your address when they come."

Ayşe, thinking on her feet again, made up a plausible-sounding address and he dutifully jotted it down on a piece of paper. We thanked the kind couple for their help and made our way outside.

"Now run, quickly," hissed Ayşe as the front door closed quietly behind us.

We ran as fast as our young legs could carry us, praying as we ran that we would not bump into the police. We stopped running only once we had left the gates of the estate behind us, and at that moment we saw a blue and white police Panda car turning in. It was only then that we started to laugh, and the hilarity lasted all the way home. Our hearts were still racing, though. I don't recall ever playing Knock Down Ginger again.

There were times that Mehmet would get my two younger brothers, Niazy and Erden, and me into the living room, close the door, get down on his knees and ask us to fight him, three against one. We would all charge like bulls at him, but he would pick us up as easily as if he were picking cherries and throw us up in the air on to the sofas – if we were lucky enough to have one positioned in our flight path. And of course, Mehmet's feats would be accompanied by loud claims that he was the king.

One day, when he made another request for a three-on-one fight, I was reluctant and refused his kind offer. "Come on, don't be a chicken," he chided. "Look, I'm on my knees, and I'll even put one hand behind my back."

Erden and Niazy launched into their usual charge, but Mehmet grabbed Erden by the front of his jumper and threw him across the room. He then caught hold of Niazy and lobbed him easily in the opposite direction. As he was throwing Niazy, I saw my chance, charged in and punched Mehmet hard on the nose.

The shock was evident on his face. "Argh! My nose!" cried the king, his throne rocking slightly beneath him.

Feri came flying in to find the cause of the commotion. "Look, it's flippin' bleeding!" screamed Mehmet. "I was play-fighting with the boys and Küfi punched me right on the nose." He felt the injured part gingerly.

The unsympathetic Feri laughed harshly. "Serves you right for picking on the kids," she sniffed.

Feri was the tough one of the girls. She loved growing her nails and wearing make-up and jewellery, albeit behind my father's back.

Thin with long brown hair and big brown eyes, she liked a good laugh and usually picked on her older sister Hicran for her entertainment. But she would fight Hicran's battles at school if anyone picked on her, scratching, punching and pulling hair. She was wild!

One day, I remember, she saw a girl kick Hicran. "Why did that girl just kick you?" she asked. "She wanted my money and I wouldn't give it to her," Hicran replied.

"Did you give it to her?" insisted Feri.

"Yes, I gave her my ten shillings. She kicked me," conceded the frightened Hicran.

Feri ran after the bully, scratched her and pulled her hair, then began banging her head on a wall. "You gonna take my sister's money, are you? Give it back now, give it back!" she screamed.

The girl was by now more than willing to give the money to Feri, who then gave it back to Hicran. "Why can't you just stick up for yourself?" she yelled. "What's the matter with you? Don't just sit back and be bullied, fight back!"

But similar scenes occurred throughout their secondary school lives, and Feri was constantly fighting the placid Hicran's battles. Now she was fighting one for me.

"Quick Küfi, come here." Feri pushed me behind her for protection from Mehmet, who was preparing to exact revenge for the damage to his nose. But that was the end of his boastful three-on-one exploits. He never challenged us again.

One summer day around that time, I was playing in the top front room where my three sisters slept. The sash windows were wide open, and I decided to climb out and sit on the windowsill, enjoying the fine, sunny weather. I looked down on the neighbourhood from my bird's eye vantage point and marvelled at how different it all looked spread out before me.

Not long before, I had watched the film *Mary Poppins* and admired the heroine's aeronautical skills with an umbrella. Surely, I reasoned, if I got an umbrella and jumped, it would act like a parachute, just as it did for the magical nanny.

"What you doin'?" asked Niazy, who had entered the room behind me.

"Nothin', just sittin' 'ere," I replied casually.

"Move over then." My brother clambered out to join me on the sill.

Niazy was the cute, skinny, athletic one, with light fine brown straight hair. He was Feri's little favourite and she often tried to upset him almost to the point of tears, because she loved the way his chin would wobble. She would then smother him with hugs and kisses to stop him actually crying.

Within minutes Erden had climbed out to join us, and all three of us sat on the first-floor windowsill, our legs dangling in the South London air.

Suddenly, "don't move!" came a panicky voice from the street. Then Feri came out of the house and saw the three of us chatting away on the windowsill. "Oh my God! Don't move a muscle, stay still!" she screamed, pulling at her hair.

Soon, quite a crowd had gathered beneath us. "Are you OK?" called Feri.

"Yeah," we replied, casually and simultaneously. What, we wondered, was all the fuss about?

"Oh, that's good," said Feri, forcing some calmness into her voice. "Just stay still and be good boys."

Whoosh! The next thing we knew, all three of us had been snatched back through the window by Hicran and Mehmet, and given the mother and father of all tickings-off.

Still, for the following few years, I continued to wonder whether it would be possible to float down from that window with a standard issue black umbrella. They should have given *Mary Poppins* a '15' certificate.

We really appreciated each other's company as children; material things didn't matter at all. We didn't have any fancy toys and most of our clothes were hand-me-downs from older brothers or sisters. I guess Erden, being the youngest, must have worn clothes that had passed through four brothers before ending up on him.

Erden was the clumsy one. Give him a glass of milk and he would spill it, drop it, harm himself with it, or even endanger anyone unlucky enough to be near him. He was really a smaller version of me, dark brown hair with brown eyes, but very slight as a child.

He had to be watched over at all times by the older children. Crossing the road would be a problem as he had already been knocked over by a car. Leaving medication within his reach would be a bad move as he had already downed a whole pot of tablets before being rushed to hospital to have his stomach pumped. Give him money and he'd no doubt swallow it. This kid could do damage if you gave him a feather to play with.

But Erden was Hicran's favourite, and she usually took care of him while Mum and Dad were working. In fact, we all kind of paired up: Mehmet and İlker, Hicran and Feri, Ayşe and me, Niazy and Erden; this was the usual grouping when we played together.

The girls' chores consisted of feeding the younger boys and cleaning the house. We didn't have a vacuum cleaner, so the carpets were swept with a hard-brush broom and the carpeted staircase with a dustpan and brush. The girls were forever arguing over who did what and there would be hair-pulling and screaming if they could not arrive at an amicable agreement.

A typical meal consisted of tinned spaghetti with mash or chips and beans. Sundays were different, though, as Dad's fish and chip shop, the Seafare Fish Bar, did not open until 6pm. Every Sunday Mum would cook traditional Turkish food and occasionally Dad would make us shish kebabs – he had bought a gas cooker with a gadget that rotated a line of skewers under the grill.

Sundays were great. It was the only time we could sit together as a family and enjoy a feast. Dad would get out the Johnnie Walker Red Label whisky and Emva Cream Cyprus sherry for Mum – and we kids would get a sip of sherry if we were lucky. Dad only drank on Sundays, and I guess he was brought up in a time and country in which there were no restrictions on giving alcohol to children.

"Here son, have a little sip of Cyprus sherry," he would say to me in Turkish, a big smile on his face.

"No, Hassan," Mum would chide.

"It's OK, it's only sherry, it won't harm him," would be Dad's reply. And his say was always final.

"Mmm, can I have some more?" I would plead. The sherry was deliciously sweet.

"No, no more," Mum would insist.

"Leave the little man alone. He likes it," would be Dad's response, and he would laugh his head off at the thought that I liked to drink. "Aslansın! (you're a lion!)," he would add, ruffling my hair.

He believed that giving alcohol to children would prevent them from becoming alcoholics at a later age. I'm not too sure if the theory is a good one, but I guess it worked for me.

One Sunday morning after breakfast, Mum and Dad went out somewhere only to find on their return Ayşe and me sitting at the dining room table with a sherry bottle three-quarters empty. Needless to say, we were absolutely plastered, giggling and slumping all over the furniture. Dad managed to quell his laughter enough to tell us not to do it again, while Mum put us to bed to sleep it off.

Dad often brought this incident up later in life, but as usual he was unable to get his words out, laughing so much that the tears streamed down his face.

CHAPTER THREE

Turkish Cypriots immigrate to the UK

I don't know much about my father's activities in the Second World War. He used to tell me stories when I was a child but, sad to say, I can't remember them clearly, and he has now passed away. He hated talking about war but after a few shots of whisky on a Sunday he would often start to recount one of his stories – not of fighting but of his life and the nice people he had met in the prisoner of war camp.

I remember him telling me that he was captured in the first year of the war and that he spent the remaining five long years as a POW. At the time of his capture he was a sergeant with the British forces in Cyprus and, as far as I understand, he was imprisoned in Germany.

He tried to get on with certain German guards; some of them were nice guys, he explained, and they liked him as he had made the effort to learn to communicate in their language. The camp was 'home' to both English and Russian POWs and Dad was taught to play the violin by an English musician.

He recounted once how he made an attempt to escape, giving some cigarettes to a guard and asking him to open the gates so he could have a little walk outside the camp. The guard was hesitant, but he had gained my father's trust over the years – they used to chat a lot and had built up some kind of friendship. My father had no intention of escaping, he insisted; he just wanted to wander around outside the camp. Eventually the guard agreed to let him out and, needless to say, my father did not return. But he was caught the following day and promptly returned to the camp.

At the end of the war Dad returned to Cyprus, but he was in for a shock. When he returned home, his son Uner, who was about seven at the time, refused to believe that he was looking at his father. "My dad has a moustache," he insisted. My father laughed and spent the next few weeks growing a moustache so his son would believe it was him.

I'm not too sure how Dad came to the UK but I believe it was when he left the British forces; they asked him where he would like to go and he said the UK. He was sent at first to London but ended up in Wales for a while.

He told me once that he met an old lady who used to ask him around to her house for tea; apparently he was the spitting image of her son, who had died in the war. Their relationship as friends grew strong and the lady helped him to settle down in the UK. I believe Dad worked in a factory making parts of some sort.

He was once invited by the lady, whom he now called 'mum', to have tea with a politician she knew well as she was helping in his election campaign. She introduced my father to Clement Attlee, the Labour Party leader at the time. Attlee shook my father's hand but there was not much chat between the two of them as Dad did not speak much English at that time.

After tea the lady told my father that Mr Attlee would be the next Prime Minister, but Dad refused to believe that was possible; Churchill had won the war and that alone would keep him in office. The lady smiled at him: "You wait and see," she replied.

By the time Mr Attlee had made it into office, my father had already left for London and had lost touch with the kind lady. She was a very nice woman, he said, and he regretted losing contact with her, but he had felt bad at the time as she would do anything for him – just because he looked like her son.

My father was a strong-minded and sometimes stubborn man, but he was always very gentle with his children and never laid a finger on us when we were naughty. On one occasion Niazy, at the age of two, got on to a chair in the kitchen and started throwing plates on the floor, laughing every time one smashed. My mother screamed for help from my father, who joined my brother in laughing at the scene. "Leave him alone, he's having fun," he chortled as mum desperately tried to stop yet another of her plates hitting the deck.

I remember that when he had his chip shop in Tooting, Dad would often have drunks and trouble-makers coming in, and he would always protect us by confronting them fearlessly, and physically pushing them out of the shop. He really was not afraid of anybody, even in his old age.

Mother was sent to the UK in 1956 at the age of sixteen by her parents, who had arranged her marriage to Ali in the UK. Her older sister was already married and living in London, so my mother was the second child, out of the seven children in her family, to come to the UK. During the sea voyage to Britain she was looked after by a Greek couple, she remembered.

Mother married and had five children: İlker and Mehmet (boys), Hicran, Feriha and Ayşe (girls). But her husband was violent and beat her constantly, even when she was pregnant, with the result that she had several miscarriages.

By the time Ayşe was about a year old Mother had at last left her husband, but she was forced to leave the two older boys and two girls in a Catholic home. Of course, she visited them often until she met my father Hassan, who helped to get the children out by offering to help support them.

At the time he owned a house in North London and had been letting rooms out, and one of them was rented by a Greek woman with whom Mother had made friends. After visiting her friend several times, Mother was introduced to my father and with time they became friends and ended up living together.

I believe my father sold the house for something like £1,800 and bought a chip shop with accommodation above in Shuttleworth Road, East Ham. The business did not do well and we ended up at Darren Buildings, a halfway house on York Road, Battersea for about a year before being given a council house in Kenilford Road, Balham.

Darren Buildings was a Victorian building that was four or five storeys high and ran along York Road, next to Price's candle factory. It was not well maintained and had not been brought up do date: the flats had neither bathroom nor toilet.

In the middle of the building was a drive-through entrance, which led to a very large space that contained two rows of garages, back to back. Why they had built garages there was a mystery to me, for there were never any cars. The families placed in Darren Buildings couldn't afford them.

Dad had found work and would labour long hours in a fish and chip shop, while İlker, at the age of fourteen, had his first job doing paper rounds for a newsagent.

İlker saved his money up and bought us all small gifts for Christmas that year, 1968. His gift for me was a battery-operated robot, the first electronic toy I'd ever had. He would switch the robot on from across the room and it would start to walk towards me with lights flashing from its eyes and stomach area. I would laugh then scream, running for cover behind Mum or Dad as it got closer.

That was the first and last Christmas gift I had until I reached my teenage years for Dad, being a Muslim, didn't allow us to celebrate the festival. In nursery or primary school as Christmas was approaching, I was always baffled when everyone else talked about the gifts they'd asked Santa for. Once, when I was asked what I would like for Christmas, the teacher answered the children on my behalf, saying I was a Muslim and Muslims didn't celebrate Christmas. That was when I really understood why I was so different to the rest of the kids.

One day, on our father's birthday, Feri wanted to surprise Mum and Dad by getting up early to make them breakfast in bed. She lit the gas stove and put the steel kettle on. Not being able to reach the grill, she climbed on a chair to make some toast.

As she leaned forward to turn over the slices of bread, Feri's nightie caught alight from the flames that were heating the kettle. As she began to scream for help, the kettle started to whistle. Dad came charging into the kitchen and leapt to put the blaze out with his bare hands, then wrapped a tea towel around Feri to stifle the flames.

"What were you doing, darling?" he cried.

"I was making you and Mummy breakfast in bed for your birthday, Daddy," Feri replied, the tears still flowing.

Dad's eyes welled up and his tears joined Feri's. He had got there just in time and Feri had not suffered any burns.

"Thank you, darling, but you must not do that again," he sobbed. "It's very dangerous to use the cooker. You could have been burnt very badly." He hugged his daughter as the tears continued to run.

I remember Mum's sister and brother-in-law, who lived in Bournemouth, visiting us. They had brought with them a tricycle that one of their children had grown out of, to give to me.

It was a good, old-fashioned trike with a green frame and a big white front wheel and two slightly smaller wheels at the rear. The handle bars were silver with white rubber handles, and the well-padded seat had springs underneath for extra comfort. I would often ride the trike in the courtyard outside our flat.

One sunny day Hicran saw a crowd of kids outside, riding their bikes. "Everyone come and line up against this wall. We're going to have a race!" she announced.

All the kids rushed over with their bikes and lined up against the wall. There must have been about fifteen of us lined up, with a wide range in age and bike sizes.

"Right, I want you all to race all the way down the yard, up along the right of the garages, around the back and back down the other side to here," ordered Hicran "The first one back will be the winner."

Suddenly, a little boy to my right, about four bikes away, started to cry. The boy next to him started to weep, then the next boy along began to bawl. It was obviously contagious, for within seconds I was crying myself. There must have been six of us, all sobbing our hearts out. Hicran, mystified, asked the first boy why he was crying but couldn't get any sense out of him. Giving up, she came over to me.

"Küfi, why are you crying?" she asked.

"Because he's crying." I pointed at the boy next to me.

"OK, everybody stop crying now or we won't have this race!" shouted Hicran. Silence descended swiftly. "Good! Now are you all ready?"

We nodded, putting our feet on our right pedals. "Ready, steady, go!" yelled Hicran and we were away, pedalling furiously.

By the time I had reached the first garage the others were already making their way back. I thought it pointless to carry on, so I just turned and made my way back to join the others.

Darren Buildings housed the poor and those addicted to drugs and alcohol. I recall two particularly tragic incidents during our time there.

Once, a newborn baby was put in one of the large steel cylindrical community bins, then the rubbish was set alight. Everyone could hear the baby's screams and many rushed to help, but there was nothing they could do as the flames engulfed the bin. The fire brigade arrived but it was way too late; the baby had been burned to death.

Men, women and children were in utter shock. But this happened twice during the year that we were living at Darren Buildings.

CHAPTER FOUR

A step back in time

Our little family group – my mother, brothers Niazy (then aged seven) and Erden (five) and I – collected our luggage and made our way towards the airport exit through customs control. We were met by a man dressed in a uniform with a flat army-style hat. He started asking my mother questions in Greek.

Although Mother was Turkish, she knew some Greek as she had mixed with Greek children and learned the language when she was growing up. The island of Cyprus has had a mixed Greek-Turkish population for hundreds of years, and they had mostly got on well and learned each other's languages.

The officer's manner was abrupt. "Why have you come here?" he demanded to know.

"We've come to see my mother and father," replied Mum.

"There is trouble here," advised the officer. "You should go back to London."

The Green Line

But Mum was not to be deterred. "No, I want to see my parents," she insisted. "I'm not worried, so let us through."

I remember the anger that distorted the officer's face as he stamped Mother's passport and waved us through. He would have preferred that wave, I felt sure, to be a blow aimed at any one of us. As it was, he contented himself with confiscating Mother's two cartons of duty free cigarettes, which she had bought for Granddad, and telling her she could have them back on her return journey to the UK.

I had no understanding of Greek, but my young senses told me there was a problem. "What was the matter, Mummy?" I asked as we hurried away from the confrontation.

"It's OK," said my mother casually. "Some Greeks just don't like Turkish people."

This was the first I'd heard about friction between Greeks and Turks. I remembered that my father had many Greek friends with whom he got on very well, but I realised later why he hadn't wanted us to go on this holiday.

Dad was one of those people who would never miss the TV news broadcasts. As he couldn't read he never bought newspapers, but he always watched the news – and only the news – on TV, and listened to radio broadcasts from Turkey every Sunday. He knew something that Mother could not quite comprehend, but she could not be talked out of travelling to see her parents again, no matter what rumours were flying around.

We walked out of the airport building and found a taxi to take us to a small village called İpsillat, which has since been renamed Sütlüce. This was where my grandparents and aunt were living. I found out later that my grandparents had lived previously in a neighbouring town called Lefkoniko by the Greeks and Lefkonuk by the Turks (it's now been renamed Geçitkale). It's to the north-east of Nicosia, on the way to the Peninsula, a finger of land that points towards the Turkish mainland town of Samandag.

Sadly, the grandparents had to leave their home in Lefkonuk as a result of the troubles between the Turkish people and EOKA, which wanted Cyprus to be unified with Greece. The Turks of Lefkonuk, I learned, received clear threats forcing them to leave the town and, once they had left, their homes were razed to the ground.

"İpsillat, lütfen (İpsillat, please)," my mother requested the taxi driver.

"Tamam, binin araba'ya (OK, get in the car)," he replied in Turkish.

The driver placed our luggage in the spacious boot of his Mercedes and set off. The journey to İpsillat was a pleasant one. The car's windows were wound all the way down and although the breeze ruffling our hair was very warm, at least it cooled us down a little.

But as well as being a nice ride, for us boys the journey was a real eye-opener. The scenery was a completely new experience, the arid landscape leading to the beautiful Kyrenia mountain range to the left of us, all the way to our destination. We'd never seen mountains before. Well, we were unlikely to come across mountains in South London.

"Are we going to go up the mountains, Mum?" I asked, my stomach knotted in excitement.

"No, but your grandparents live not too far from them," she replied.

"So, can we walk up the mountains then?"

"Maybe. I don't see why not, but you'll have to be careful," Mum warned. "There are a lot of snakes living on the mountains."

Snakes? This was something else that we hadn't come across in Balham. "Wow!" we all three replied, wide-eyed.

We made a left turn on to a narrow road that would only take one and a half cars side by side, at a squeeze. Every time a car approached our taxi from the opposite direction, its driver and ours would slow down and manoeuvre their vehicles, half on the road, half on the roadside dirt track, in order to pass safely. Used to London's broad and bustling thoroughfares, we watched each manoeuvre with trepidation and fascination.

On the way to İpsillat the road passed through several villages, which effectively prepared us for the kind of place we were heading for. To our young eyes, the houses looked incredibly old and run down. We passed odd-looking shops without the familiar glass frontages, and cafés where old men sat on chairs made from wood and hand-woven straw, drinking coffee from tiny cups.

Although the weather struck us as searingly hot, the men wore trousers, long-sleeved shirts and jackets as they sat outside the cafés playing backgammon, chatting loudly, emphasising their points with expansive hand gestures and slamming the backgammon pieces aggressively down into the box to show opponents and spectators they were playing a serious game. In the near-empty streets, the women were dressed in long-sleeved tops, long skirts or flowery dresses, and their hair was covered with headscarves. This was a very different style to the mini skirts, platform shoes, wide collars and flared trousers that were fashionable in London at the time.

It took no more than a few seconds to pass through each tiny village. In between these settlements lay expanses of flat, arid, open farmland with the occasional, still-as-stone tree breaking the horizon. As we gazed through the taxi's windscreen, we could see waves of hot air shimmering and dancing above the hot tarmac.

We were approaching İpsillat. As the village came into view, we made out the shapes of a few men who seemed to be blocking the road. Closer inspection confirmed that it was indeed a blockade and the car came to a halt next to a tall, slender cabin on the side of the road, similar to the sentry boxes I'd seen outside Buckingham Palace. A police officer stepped briskly out of the box and approached our taxi. He was the bearer of unwelcome news.

"You can't enter the village," the tall, broad-shouldered man in uniform informed us. "You will have to turn back."

"But I'm dropping off my passengers," argued the taxi driver.

The policeman peered into the back of the car, where we three youngsters were wondering what on earth was going on. Nothing in our experience had prepared us for this. "Where are you going?" he asked my mother.

"I'm visiting my parents."

"Who are they?"

"Mehmet and Ayşe Salih," Mum told him. "What's the problem?"

The policeman gave no answer but parried with a question of his own: "The driver is Greek; why did you choose a Greek taxi?"

"How was I to know he was Greek?" answered my mother. "He speaks fluent Turkish."

In response to the policeman's demand that we get out of the car, we all scrambled out on to the roadside and the men took our luggage from the boot. Mother paid the driver and he turned his car round and drove off without a word. Not surprisingly, he seemed quite anxious to get away.

"Don't you recognise me?" the man in uniform asked Mother. She scrutinised his dark, handsome features but drew a blank. "I'm Erdal, your cousin. Leave your bags here and get down to your parents' house. I'll get my men to bring your luggage later."

My mother was flustered. "Oh, how are you and your family?" she asked. "Sorry, I really didn't recognise you."

"They're all fine," Erdal assured her. "Go now, and we'll talk later."

Wondering silently what adventures and dangers lay before us, we set off and were at my grandparents' house in no time. Once inside, we kids once again encountered something new: greeting our elderly relatives, we were told to kiss the backs of their hands and place them on our foreheads. This was the customary sign of respect to one's elders. Grandma, meanwhile, could not stop kissing and hugging us, overcome as she was with happiness to see us. Grandma was very short, but large, with a wrinkled face that had happiness lines running from the sides of her eyes. She had few teeth so her lips were drawn into her mouth, but she wore a constant smile.

Her skin was tanned by the fierce sun and her grey hair –three-quarters covered by a headscarf with little round balls of cotton sewn round the edges – had tones of orange from the henna she used to dye it. Like many Turkish women she loved her gold, and on her wrist clanked a profusion of golden bangles . Her clothing was simple: long skirt, loose top, a pair of slippers.

As I inspected my new surroundings in the house and outside, I had the extraordinary feeling that I had stepped back a hundred years in time. On the village's dirt roads, occasional passers-by riding donkeys raised thick clouds of dust. The little house had no lights and, even in daytime, seemed gloomy to someone who was used to the bright lights of Balham. The floors were laid, far from evenly, with stone slabs and the walls were made from mud and straw bricks that were rendered with cement and plastered haphazardly on the inside.

The Green Line

There was no TV – quite a shock for us London kids – and the house's only electrical appliance was in the living room: a fridge-freezer whose large metal handle was wrapped with cloth. My puzzled questions about the cloth were answered: you were in danger of electrocution if you weren't careful when opening the door.

To my surprise, the beds, made of black-painted metal frames and metal spring bases, were also in the living room. There was an unusual, pervasive smell of damp, dust and mothballs.

Yet it was not at all difficult to adjust to these unfamiliar surroundings. It had not been too long since we had found ourselves living in that halfway home, Darren Buildings. The ten of us had inhabited two two-bedroom flats that boasted neither bathroom nor toilet. We had had to wash in tin baths set on the living room floor, and we had shared an outdoor toilet with others in the block of flats.

So, although life in İpsillat certainly provided us with a change of environment, it didn't strike us kids as too drastic a change. And hey, we were on holiday and we were going to have a great time. Nothing could possibly spoil our fun …

CHAPTER FIVE

Cyprus life

It was hot, hot, oh so hot, and we were nowhere near prepared for it, wearing clothes that weren't even suitable for an English summer. A lady called at our nan's house with a suitcase in hand – still quite a common sight in Cyprus, where travelling sales people call now and again in the hope of selling you their goods. My brothers and I were given the more suitable attire of shorts, vests and flip-flops.

That was all we really needed, but it was weird wearing flip-flops for the first time: the plastic thong that goes between the big and second toes cut into my skin painfully at first. With time and use, however, the skin hardened and the pain disappeared.

This was, of course, our first meeting with our auntie and cousins. Cousin Mustafa, aged nine, tall, thin and tanned with short, straight black hair and a permanent grin, pulled us away from the elders at Nan's house and dragged us to his home, a few doors away. On the way, my brothers and I saw that some kid must have dropped their chocolate sweets on the road.

"Yum, Maltesers!" cried young Erden, bending to pluck one of the prized treats from its dusty resting place.

"Yok! Yapma! (No! Don't do it!)" yelled Mustafa, pulling Erden up by the hand that was about to close on its prize.

"It's OK," grumbled Erden. "I was going to blow the dust off."

"Nedir? (what is it?)" asked Mustafa, the widest of grins on his face.

I couldn't believe our cousin wasn't familiar with Maltesers. "They're delicious, round balls of chocolate with honeycomb centres," I explained.

Mustafa's laughter rang through the street. "They're not delicious," he spluttered, "they're goat droppings."

It took a second, but then we, too, started laughing. The closer we looked at the objects in question, the more they really did resemble Maltesers.

Our cousins' home turned out to be much nicer than Nan's, with marble-effect floors and walls made from real bricks. They even had a television, so you can imagine where we spent most of our time while we were in İpsillat.

Later that day, Mustafa showed us round the village. Having crossed over a dried-out canal and passed the mosque opposite Mustafa's house, we stumbled on five soldiers sitting outside a small building, playing backgammon and drinking Turkish coffee. Our cousin greeted them and introduced us to the soldiers.

These men, he explained later, were Turkish Cypriot soldiers called Mujahit. A very small force with limited weapons, they would have no chance against the Greeks in protecting the Turkish population if war ever broke out, he confided. All they did was play backgammon and drink the thick black coffee all day.

We continued our tour and after about three minutes came to the edge of the village. How small İpsillat seemed compared to the endless cityscape of our home.

At the edge of İpsillat was the Kahve (coffee house), where the men and boys of the village gathered to chat, play backgammon, table football or cards and drink alcohol, coffee or pop. We pulled up some seats and ordered Coca-Cola and Bubble Up (a Turkish Cypriot soda drink, an imitation of 7 Up), which came in old recycled glass bottles with wax-coated paper straws.

We sat there for a good while, watching the occasional antiquated vehicle pass by on the dirt road and taking in the arid landscape and new smells that hung in the air. Even the sounds around us seemed a world away from those of London.

Mustafa explained that the Greeks and Turks had not been getting on since Britain had granted independence to Cyprus in 1960. "The situation has been getting worse by the day," he sighed. "Greeks and Turks lived on this island for hundreds of years in absolute harmony. Christians and Muslims living together, working together, socialising together: what a wonderful story about our paradise island was being told to the world.

"Then came EOKA, which was a Greek Cypriot party that fought to get rid of British troops and Turks from the island and wanted 'enosis', union with Greece. The Greeks

The Green Line

say Cyprus is their island, that they were here before the Turkish."

"Is that true?" I asked.

"I don't know, but the island had been ruled by many countries throughout its history." Mustafa went on to name some of those rulers. "The Egyptians, Phoenicians, Persians, Romans and Ottomans, to name just a few."

"Yeah, my dad told me the Ottomans rented the island to the British in 1878," I recalled. "But, because Turkey fought on the Germans' side in the First World War, they decided to take over the island completely, until they left in 1960. They'd had enough of the trouble caused by the Greeks who wanted them out."

"Yes, that's right, they teach us all of this at school," confirmed Mustafa, sucking some Coke up his straw. His face brightened. "Let's play table football."

The four of us went to the table and frantically spun the handles of the rods on which the plastic footballers were standing to attention. It was free to play and we had enormous fun for over an hour, shouting, screaming and laughing, before dragging our feet homewards.

In our grandparents' garden was a large dome-shaped clay oven. Nan filled it with dried branches and small pieces of log, set them alight and waited until the flames had died down, leaving red hot glowing embers. She then placed a large round stainless steel roasting pan, filled with chicken pieces, potatoes, cut onions and tomato purée, in the oven. A small olive branch, placed inside to one side, was, I guess, to flavour the food with its smoke. Nan then covered the front opening of the oven with a heavy iron square plate, securing its position with large rocks.

The food smelled unbelievably great and tasted amazing. We feasted on the scorching hot food with fresh Turkish bread, dipping it in the juices on our plates, then, finishing off with refreshing, sweet watermelon.

Nan, a fantastic cook, was forever in the kitchen, working away at keeping us fed. My favourites were her böreks (fried pastry with either minced lamb and onion or halloumi and onion in the middle). She would make platefuls of these and we would nibble at them throughout the day, morning, noon and night. She also made bread at times, and the house would always be filled with enticing aromas.

Another novelty for us London kids was the sight of the chickens that roamed around in the gardens and even out on the streets. Nan had quite a few, so we always had fresh eggs – and fresh chicken, for that matter. She also had a couple of goats which she would milk every morning, sitting on a makeshift stool, placing a pan underneath and pulling away at the udders.

One morning she asked me if I wanted to have a go. She put me into position, took my hands and placed them on a goat's udder. "Şimdi çek memeleri (now pull the teats)," she instructed.

I pulled and squeezed, pulled and squeezed again and pulled and squeezed harder, only for the goat to turn its head and regard me with a cheesed-off expression. Pull and squeeze as I might, I couldn't force a single drop of milk out. I took the decision to give up; the goat looked so frustrated that I was sure it was about to go on the attack. Nan laughed and told me it would take time to learn.

Nan was a real village woman, small but tough. She would take an axe and chop wood for ages without stopping once for a breather. I tried to match her feats, but again without success

We were soft city kids compared to the people out here. Back home, chicken came packed from the butcher and milk was bottled and delivered by the milkman.

We three boys and our cousin Mustafa played together from dawn to dusk, spending most of our time playing on the table football at the coffee bar. The village was peaceful apart from the early mornings, when the cockerels would crow in every garden. You didn't need an alarm clock or a watch out here; time was measured by the sun's position, the sound of the cockerels and the wildlife.

The days were extremely hot and the nights seemed much cooler, with the odd welcomed breeze. Looking up at the night sky I was amazed by the clusters of stars that were visible.

Unlike the London sky, normally overcast but with a handful of stars on view when it was clear, the Cyprus heavens were always clear and you could see millions of stars, most of them clustered together. There was hardly any light pollution in the village, just the occasional dim streetlight positioned here and there.

I was fascinated by the stars and spent many a night just gazing up at their beauty. By night as well as by day, this place truly was a paradise.

CHAPTER SIX

Samson in power

Our first few blissful days in İpsillat were spent playing marbles, riding (and falling off) bikes and generally joking around. But I was keen to discover more about this strange new world, and asked Granddad if I could go out with him one morning to tend his sheep.

I was woken at four in the morning by my mother, who was holding an oil lamp. I was given a packed lunch of olive bread and water, a hat and a long stick to help me control the sheep, and was warned to keep an eye out for snakes. Granddad and I then set off to the fields with about twenty sheep.

I saw how Granddad placed his long stick horizontally across the backs of his shoulders, then drooped his arms over the ends of the stick. Following behind, I did exactly the same with my stick. It felt good; my arms felt weightless and I guess it helped me look the part.

Granddad, born in the late 1890s and therefore well into his seventies, looked even more ancient to my eyes. His hair, short, pure white and balding at the crown, contrasted sharply with his dark complexion. He was tall and thin, and he looked frail. An eye operation years before had not gone well, and he had ended up with permanently squinting eyes, one smaller than the other.

We walked and walked, and then walked some more. Eventually, it was light and Granddad was happy that the area we found ourselves in was good enough for the sheep to feed in. He told me to eat my olive bread, drink some water and have a nap. While he had no problem sleeping for about two hours, there was no way I could drop off – especially with the thought that there might be snakes in the field whirling round my head.

I sat up, watched the sheep grazing and kept up a constant vigil for snakes. What should an eight-year-old boy do when he sees a snake for the first time? Hit it with a stick, run or just scream? I wasn't required to do anything with the sheep, which stayed together in a tightly packed bunch. Perhaps they were as scared of snakes as I was.

Being a shepherd in Cyprus was extremely dangerous as well as boring, I decided, and when we returned home that afternoon I vowed to myself that my first experience of shepherding would also be my last. Still, it would be something to tell the kids back home.

"Did you enjoy it?" chorused Mum and Nan.

"Yeah, it was OK," I lied.

"That's good," smiled Mum, "you can help your granddad again tomorrow."

The next morning she did her best to wake me, but there was no way in the world I was going to budge.

Nothing, absolutely nothing, was going to get me out of bed to sleep in that field of creepy, crawly snakes.

One day was spent at the beach in Kyrenia, and even that was an unusual experience. The sand was beautiful, but it was also so hot that you had to run fast to get to the safety of the sea, or risk your feet being burned. My brothers and I screamed with every step, and I'm sure I remember seeing steam rising from our feet when we reached the water.

But oh, that water was amazing, beautifully warm and so clear I could see little fish swimming around my feet. I'd never seen anything like it before, and it confirmed my belief that we were having the greatest holiday ever.

The next day we caught a bus to take us to the big city, Nicosia. The vehicle turned out to be an old Bedford, green and beige on the outside, cream on the inside with red seats. Boasting around thirty seats, it resembled a box with wheels. It also had a ladder at the side, to facilitate the hauling of luggage up on to the roof, and light bulbs set into the ceiling, just like the ones on the old London buses.

This bus deposited us safely in Nicosia, which was as different to my grandparents' village as it was possible to be. Unlike the near-silent, dusty streets of İpsillat, Nicosia's bustling thoroughfares were thronged with people getting on with their daily lives, and the noise was more like what we were used to in England.

Our first stop was a visit to Mother's cousin's wife, Besime, with whom we had come to Cyprus. She stayed

The Green Line

with her mother, who lived in the Orta Köy district of the city, and had a son my age. From the start I got on well with Ozzy (his shortened nickname).

We had met Ozzy for the first time a few years earlier, back in London. He and his two older brothers had introduced us to rock and roll, for they were Teddy boys and rockabillies, with slicked-back quiffs and DAs (Duck's Arse hair styles – combed in towards a centre parting at the back of the head). They wore drainpipe jeans with large, metal-buckled belts and blue suede crêpe-soled shoes. Their shirts were always left wide open at the top to display their chests and bootlace ties.

If we were already wild, Ozzy and his brothers taught us to become even wilder. They would come round to our house early in the morning and get us to go with them to our neighbours' houses, take the bottles of milk off their doorsteps and put them outside houses that did not have milk delivered. We found it hilarious to imagine the reaction of those who were expecting a delivery and those who weren't.

If we went to the park, one of us would always end up in the pond. We would play dare, lying down on the road and cheating death by scrambling to our feet when the approaching car was a few feet away.

The brothers' prize possession was a Ouija board. Making our way up to the dimly lit attic, we would sit around the board and start, with trepidation, to make contact with ghosts. Naturally, with no real ghosts willing to manifest themselves, the brothers would pick on one of our little group and make the sliding pointer select his initials. The tension would build to such a pitch that eventually, scared out of our wits, we'd plunge out of the attic, pushing each other out of the way in our determination not to be the last man out.

Now we were reunited with Ozzy. Either side of the narrow road in which he lived were houses of every shape and size imaginable. Besime's mother lived on the top floor of a house, and the access was via a concrete staircase leading from the front door. Some of the houses on the street had a pavement outside, some were high and wide, others low and narrow. The challenge of walking on the pavement from one end of the road to the other was a tricky one, so most people solved the problem by walking in the road.

One of our favourite pastimes consisted of sitting outside Ozzy's nan's house, perched on the high pavement with our feet on the road. Once we watched fascinated as three middle-aged women, sitting across the road on ancient wooden chairs, removed the leaves from bundles of mullahiya stalks. (This is a spinach-like plant, available in the Cyprus summer, whose leaves have a slightly bitter taste.) Stripping away the leaves individually but with amazing speed, the women placed the leaves in a basket and managed to carry on a non-stop gossip session at the same time.

A few doors away sat an old lady dressed in black from head to toe. I watched as she sat quietly picking at a plate of grapes, chewing the juicy morsels and then spitting the seeds on to the road. She was sitting with her legs apart but fully covered by her ankle-length skirt and her back was arched forward and her face covered in hundreds of wrinkles. Each line must have held the secret of a story from a particular period of her life.

I was also fascinated to see that there was a black couple living a few doors away from Ozzy's nan's house. The man was in his early twenties, smart and clean cut, and his wife was stunningly pretty. They had no children, and I guess that was why we didn't get to know them well.

Ozzy had an uncle called Çakmak Dayı (Uncle Lighter – as in cigarette lighter), a name that I found incredibly funny. He was a huge attraction for the local kids, for he was the proud owner of a moped and often gave the kids rides before he left for work.

It seemed an eternity before it was my turn, but at last the day dawned. Scrambling up behind Uncle Lighter, I clung to his shirt as tightly as my young hands would allow me while he tootled up and down the street. This was something that I could not imagine happening back in London, and it put a smile on my face for the rest of the day.

Meanwhile, Ozzy had introduced my brothers and me to his friends on his street – and they were delighted in telling us about the trouble between Greeks and Turks that seemed to be looming.

"We might be at war soon, and we'll kick the Greeks' arses," asserted one of the boys in Turkish.

"Don't worry, it'll be all right," Ozzy assured me, reverting to English. "We probably won't be here. We'll be flying back to London in a few days."

We sat down on the raised pavement outside Ozzy's nan's house and Ozzy pulled a matchbox from his pocket.

"What you doing wiv dat?" I asked in my best South London vernacular.

"I'll show you," he replied proudly. "I collect queen ants." Ozzy opened the box slowly to reveal two large specimens inside, snapping it shut before the trapped insects could escape.

"Help me find some more and I'll show you what I do," he urged conspiratorially. Before long, Erden and Niazy had spotted a large queen ant and pointed it out to Ozzy, who quickly deposited it in the matchbox prison.

"Now watch," he muttered as he pulled out a match from his pocket.

"You not gonna burn them alive are you?" I asked, horrified.

"Yep," replied Ozzy casually. He struck the match and set the closed box alight. "That's how I've been keeping myself busy over the last few days."

"You're wicked," cried my brothers, aghast as they watched the desperate ants wriggling in their matchbox coffin.

Ozzy's eyes widened as the poor, assassinated insects stopped moving, then a big grin spread over his face. But our attention was grabbed by a young boy who was running towards us, carrying a newspaper in one hand

and pointing to the face of a man on the front page with the other. "Nikos Sampson has taken over the government," he yelled excitedly, "and he wants to get rid of us all!"

The boy had a huge smile on his face. "We'll show him who's toughest!" he cried.

"Looks like we're at war," sighed Ozzy, reverting to English. Mum hurried out of the house and told us to get ready to leave. We were going back to the village. I guess she believed it would be safer there.

CHAPTER SEVEN

History before my eyes

My brothers and I were too young to understand fully what was happening on the political front, but our new friends were never slow to feed us scraps of information. It was not until much later in life that we read and learned more about the political instability in Cyprus in the years leading up to our 1974 visit.

There are two sides to every story, and Cypriots of Greek and Turkish origins will always recount contradictory versions of those troubled times and the island's political history. There will always be those who disagree with the stories I absorbed from my informants, the events I witnessed first hand in 1974 and, later, read about in my researches.

As I write this, thirty-seven years have passed since that momentous year. I do not mention dates as I kept no diary as the events unfolded before my wondering eyes. I have done some research to pinpoint them, but dates do not matter, and neither do the politics.

The Green Line

I do not take sides as I write; these are my honest recollections of what I, an eight-year-old boy caught in the middle of a war, experienced. The memories have never left my mind, and they are as clear as I write this as the day they were created. They always bubble to the surface of my consciousness whenever the year 1974 is mentioned, and if they have not faded in the last thirty-seven years I don't suppose they will ever disappear for good. They do not haunt me, and they never have; they are just the memories of an unfortunate period in my life to which I, as a child, adapted automatically. Amazing as it may seem now, I accepted each incident as representative of normal daily life.

As far as I know, in the spring of 1974, Cypriot intelligence found evidence that EOKA was planning a coup and was being supplied, controlled and funded by the military government in Athens. EOKA was banned, but its operations continued underground.

Archbishop Makarios, the Greek Cypriot president and leader of the Orthodox Church, wrote to the president of Greece demanding that the remaining 650 Greek officers assigned to the National Guard be withdrawn. He also accused the junta of plotting against his life and against the government of Cyprus. Makarios sent his letter to the Greek president on 2 July 1974; the reply came thirteen days later, not in the form of a letter but in an order from Athens to the Cypriot National Guard to overthrow its commander-in-chief and take control of the island.

Makarios narrowly escaped death in the attack by the Greek-led National Guard, fleeing the presidential palace and making his way to Paphos. A British helicopter took him to the Sovereign Base Area at Akrotiri, from where the Archbishop was flown to London.

In the meantime, the notorious EOKA terrorist Nikos Sampson, who was responsible for the murders of many British and Turkish Cypriots in the 1950s and 1960s, was declared provisional president of the new government. This ties in with the exact time the young boy ran to us with the newspaper informing us that Sampson had overthrown the government.

I read later that Turkey strongly believed Greece was behind all that was happening in Cyprus, so the Turkish armed forces were put on full alert. The Turkish Prime Minister, Bülent Ecevit, flew to London to ask the British government to intervene in a joint effort in its capacity as a guarantor power, but they declined to take action. Turkish warships were already at sea.

Ecevit then made a call from London to Turkey saying: "Ayşe is going on vacation," which was the code for "attack". The Turkish intervention in Cyprus began early on 20 July 1974.

As soon as we arrived at my grandparents' house in İpsillat, news reached our ears that three nearby Turkish Cypriot-occupied villages had been captured by the Greek army. Desperate for more news, my mother turned on the radio.

The Green Line

We listened, stunned, as a stern voice crackled in broken Turkish from the aged device: "All people in the village of İpsillat are asked to surrender and gather at the coffee house at the edge of the village. Do this and you will not be harmed."

The truth sank in: the Greek army had taken over the Turkish radio station – and my half-brother Üner was a news broadcaster at that very station. A million thoughts raced through our heads but we clung to one of them: maybe the troubles had persuaded him not to go to work that day.

The unwelcome message was repeated several times. As we listened and did our best to digest the news, the equally unwelcome crackle and boom of distant guns and bombs filtered into the house.

My mother turned to Nan with fear in her eyes. "What shall we do?" she cried.

"Don't believe what the radio says about being safe if you surrender," insisted Nan. "They'll kill you."

Struggling to come to terms with these incomprehensible events, my brothers and I were told to hide under the beds in the front room and keep quiet.

This was some weird kind of nightmare, wasn't it? Our young minds could not comprehend how our lives had been flipped inside out in such a short space of time but, obediently, we lay still and silent on the dusty stone slab floor, our little hearts pounding away nineteen to the dozen. But reflecting on our position, I couldn't see the wisdom in hiding under a bed – wouldn't it be the first place any Greek soldier would search?

Erden managed to curb his inquisitive nature for a few minutes, but it soon got the better of him. "What's going on?" he hissed.

"There's cobwebs under here," observed Niazy in a disgusted whisper.

I was determined to keep the peace. "Just be quiet," I whispered back urgently, trying to listen in to the adult conversation.

Silence resumed its reign over the under-bed community, but the peace was broken when the front door opened suddenly. Greek Cypriot soldiers? Not yet; the outline in the doorway belonged to an older cousin, who had been conscripted as a mujahit.

He was almost breathless. "The Greeks are making their way here," he panted. "There's nothing we can do to stop them – we haven't the manpower or the weapons."

As we took in the bad news and he scanned the room, a thought struck him. "Where are the boys?" he demanded.

"Under the bed," replied his mother (our aunt), pointing out our hiding place.

"Come out from under there," urged our cousin, bending down to our level and treating our frightened faces to a reassuring smile. "You need to get away from here."

The man on the radio repeated his assurance that we would be safe if we gave ourselves up. Then a gasp rose in unison from our little group as we recognised the voice of Üner, who had been asked to repeat what the Greek soldier had been broadcasting. The idea, no doubt, was that Turkish listeners would believe they would be in good hands.

But any sense of reassurance we might have gained was shattered as Üner, grabbing his chance, blurted out: "Don't listen to them, they'll kill you all. Get out quick, get out, get ..." We could hear the terrifying sounds of a scuffle and my half-brother being forced away from the microphone. He had obviously not followed instructions, we realised. He had risked his life to save the lives of the people of İpsillat.

"Oh my God," cried my mother, distraught. "They will kill him for doing that. Oh my God!" She was now weeping hysterically.

My cousin was thinking fast. "I have to go to help the other soldiers," he said, making his way to the front door. "We will try to delay the Greeks from getting into the village, but you must all get away now."

"No, no, no!" screamed my aunt, pulling at his arm. "Don't go my son, please don't go!" Crying as hysterically as my mother, she could not bear the thought of her son laying down his life in the defence of the village.

Her words did not have the effect she wanted. Instead there was more drama to cope with as, with a sigh, my cousin suddenly crumpled and fell to the ground in a faint. Appalled, my mother, aunt and nan struggled to pick up his inert form and lay him on one of the beds.

"Oğlum! Oğlum! (My son! My son!)" cried auntie, gently slapping his face in an attempt to bring him round.

As she tried to revive the fallen mujahit, we heard the sound of a vehicle pulling up outside the house, then the sound of its horn. We opened the door to see my mother's older cousin Hasan in the driver's seat of his VW camper van, which was crammed with passengers. Every possible square inch of space had been occupied by someone desperate to escape the village.

"We're getting out of the village," shouted Hasan. "You have to get out too, right now."

"Let us come with you," pleaded mother.

Hasan gestured at the packed interior of his vehicle. "I'm sorry, but how can I? How could I possibly fit in any more people?"

Mum wrung her hands. "Then take my children," she urged.

Hasan was torn, but the hard truth was plain to see. "I'm really sorry, I couldn't even get a baby in here," he apologised.

"Please, please try!" cried mother.

Hasan's eyes filled and his tears began to fall. "What should I do?" he groaned. "These are all my relatives, I can't just kick them off to make room for someone else. Please tell me the right thing to do!"

Despite his plight, Mother's sympathy was exhausted. "Go, just go," she yelled. "We don't want your help. Leave us, go!"

But Hasan didn't leave immediately, for he did have some hopeful news to impart. "There are three buses at the end of the field," he said. "They will be there for the next ten minutes or so. They are taking women and children to another village away from the trouble. So make your way now, go quickly!"

I looked at Hasan's face and saw the guilt it betrayed. It was tearing him apart that he was going to have to leave us behind. As his parting word – "sorry" – left his lips he could not even look us in the eyes. He clunked the camper van into gear, slammed down the accelerator and drove off at great speed. I sympathised with his tightly packed passengers, being thrown about with every rattle, bend and bump.

As the camper van roared into the distance, out of the corner of my eye I glimpsed Granddad. He was hurrying towards the house, waving his walking stick in the air and shouting to Mother: "Run through the fields now, there are buses waiting."

But Mum wasn't thinking only about herself and us kids. "What about you and Mother?" she asked.

"We're staying put," Granddad puffed. "Just take the children and go now!"

Mum took a couple of seconds to make up her mind. "Come on boys, run quickly to the buses," she cried, shooing us with her hands.

We started to cross the uneven ploughed fields in the sweltering heat, and could just about make out, far ahead, the shapes of three buses. Niazy, the athletic one of us three, was making the most headway. I stayed behind Erden but kept looking back to make sure Mother was not dropping too far behind. Mum was not exactly fleet of foot, but we, too, were handicapped by our flip-flops, which slipped off our feet every few steps. The hot brown soil played its part in delaying us, burning our feet as we struggled to fit them back into our flimsy footwear. There were weeds with long spikey prickles that we unsuccessfully tried to avoid and that scratched our feet and legs during our run to the buses.

"Run faster boys, don't wait for me," yelled our mother, but we did not obey. We could not obey. There was no way in the world we could leave her behind, so we continued to make steady but slow progress.

We were only halfway across the field when we looked up and, with a sickening feeling, saw one of the buses starting to move off. Mum was frantic. "Run faster or we'll miss them all!" she screamed.

But our progress across the field hit a further setback. One of Erden's flip-flops snapped and he flung the useless object aside with disgust. This boy was capable of breaking anything. He tried to hop on one foot, with little success, and as soon as he placed the other foot on the ground the scorching soil brought a flood of wails and sobs from the poor lad.

I ran to him and told him to climb on to my back, looking back to see that Mother was still within close range. I saw with a jolt that the second bus was starting to leave.

"Niazy," I yelled, "run as fast as you can and make sure the last bus doesn't leave without us."

Niazy, his lungs bursting, put on an incredible spurt of speed, but when he was within fifty yards of the third and last bus it began to move forward with a grinding of gears and a cloud of exhaust. It seemed clear the driver was going to leave us behind.

Niazy was incredulous and angry, and started shouting and waving his arms. To our immense relief, the bus stopped and we silently thanked God for His intervention.

Some women scrambled down off the bus and begged us to hurry. With a shock, I realised I had not an ounce more strength to carry Erden. There was no alternative but for him to jump down and for me to help him hop. Niazy to the rescue: he ran back to us and helped me support Erden to the bus. Yelling at Niazy and Erden to get on, I waited for Mother to arrive, trembling and heaving with her effort, before clambering aboard.

We had made it, but now we faced another unfamiliar situation: everybody on the bus was panicking. Some of the women were crying, for they knew they were an easy target in a bus that was sitting plainly in view in the middle of extensive flat fields. The longer they were stationary, the greater chance there was of being captured or being targeted by guns or artillery. The driver needed no reminder of the perilous situation he and his passengers found themselves in. He put his foot down hard on the accelerator and we were on our way to safer territories.

"Bismillahir Rahmanir Raheem, (In the name of Allah, most gracious and most merciful)," prayed the women as we left the village behind. They were crying for the loved ones they had had to leave behind. Would they ever see them again? What would become of my grandparents? My young mind was filled with grief, terror and apprehension.

CHAPTER EIGHT

Turkey intervenes

It was a terrifying journey, and a bumpy one, but eventually we arrived in the centre of a village called Konedra (now Gönendere) and trooped nervously off the bus. The road was lined with houses on both sides. "Where do we go from here?" Mother asked the driver.

His reply was simple, firm and reassuring. "Just knock on any door and the people will let you stay in their homes until it's safe to go back," he said. "We will sound the bus horns to let you know when it's time to leave."

Mother thanked the driver and we followed her to the nearest house. A middle-aged woman answered Mother's knock. From inside the house came the clamour of a lot of people talking and, more worryingly, people crying.

"Can we please come in?" asked Mother. "We have just arrived from İpsillat."

"I'm sorry," replied the woman, obviously harassed. "My house is full and I have no more room. Try next door." She followed this bad news by shutting the door in our faces.

Mother tried another door, and once again her knock was answered by the woman of the house.

"Hello, we have just come from İpsillat." Our mother's tone was friendly and polite. "Can we please stay in your home for a while? The children are hot and very thirsty."

The woman examined us three boys for a while and, with the thought that such young guests would probably wreck her house evidently running through her mind, answered: "Sorry, I've no room. It's not easy playing host to all these people at such short notice. Try another house." Again, the door was closed abruptly.

We walked a little further down the road and tried several more houses, but the response from the householders was always the same: no room. Now we knew how Joseph and Mary felt as they pleaded with the innkeeper in Bethlehem.

It was scorchingly hot and we were drained. Nearing the end of her tether, Mother tried yet another house.

"Hello, my children are very hot and thirsty," she announced for the umpteenth time to the woman who answered the door. "Please may we use your home to rest?" She unveiled her trump card: "The boys will be well behaved. We have tried so many homes and they have no room for us."

Mother was already turning away, expecting the customary rejection, when the woman cried: "Of course you can come in! I will make room for you and your sweet children. Come, come, get out of the sun before you become ill."

The Green Line

Our despair vanished as our new host showed us into her living room, which was crowded with people sitting and chatting. We were given bread to eat and sweet rosewater to drink. We sat quietly munching and sipping, listening to the women talking about what had happened and wondering if their homes would have been destroyed by the time they returned to their village.

The discussions were interrupted by the sudden, screaming roar of aircraft engines. Mother called us over to the garden door and pointed excitedly to the fighter planes that were zooming low over our refuge. "It's the Turkish army," she cried, and everyone in the house started to cheer. "They've come to save us."

Someone turned on the radio and we heard that Turkey had intervened to help its Turkish brothers and sisters in Cyprus. Turkey, it was clear, would no longer sit back and watch Turkish Cypriots being massacred by the Greek army, even if other countries did not consent to their actions.

The warplanes flew back and forth, from the northern mountain range and over the houses, and thunderous cheers rose to greet them every time they passed near.

Turkish Cypriots called the soldiers who came from Turkey Mehmetcik (pronounced Mehmetjik and meaning Little Mehmet). As I mentioned before, the Turkish Cypriot mujahit were a very small force and had absolutely no chance of defending their people from the Greek invasion. I should point out that Archbishop Makarios himself stated in one of his letters that this was indeed a Greek invasion of the island.

We heard later that the people of the three villages that were captured by the Greeks were massacred. According to our sources, the Greeks rounded up the villagers, bound their hands and, using a bulldozer, pushed them all into a pit. The bulldozer then finished off the vile task by filling in the pit and the villagers were buried alive. This, we were told, happened in all three villages and would probably have happened to us if we had surrendered and gathered at the coffee bar, as we'd been instructed to do so many times on the radio.

You hear horror stories coming from both Greeks and Turks about horrible atrocities perpetrated during those terrifying times. My thoughts? War is an evil act unique to mankind and must always be avoided if there is any alternative of any kind whatever. Now, imagine this if you can: before your disbelieving eyes, your mother, father, sister or brother – maybe all of them – are killed by the enemy. Would it not stir up in you a hate of which you would not have thought yourself capable?

Now try this: imagine a member of your family being buried alive, or a baby brother being riddled with bullets. What would be the over-riding emotion in your mind if you had witnessed one of these things? An overwhelming desire for revenge? Most of us, I submit, would answer yes to that question. Most of us, in the heat of the moment, would do anything – even things that would have previously seemed to us wholly unthinkable – to achieve that revenge.

Revenge is a powerful and cruel master, and it's no wonder we so often hear horror stories from both warring sides in a conflict like the one that engulfed Cyprus in 1974. I would never, ever attempt, or want, to justify war crimes but I do understand why they happen. Atrocities of war have been committed since man first swung a primitive club or threw a rock in anger, and they will continue to plague us as long as the human race inhabits this planet. The potential for cruelty and evil lurks within every one of us. Can anyone say its release will never be triggered?

We had been in Konedra for around four hours when we heard the bus drivers sounding their vehicles' horns, telling us it was safe to return to our village. But what on earth, we wondered, had happened to those that had stayed? What stories were we going to hear?

Everyone boarded the buses and we set off for home. It was an uneventful journey and, on our arrival in the village, we saw with relief that all seemed to be unchanged. There were no signs of fighting, no scarred buildings, no ruined houses, no casualties. My mother, two brothers and I returned to Nan's house, where we found her busy going about her normal daily routine.

"What happened, Mother?" cried Mum, enveloping Nan in a passionate embrace.

"Oh, nothing," answered Nan casually. "The Greeks were stopped in their tracks. They didn't make it to the village."

The relief among us four was almost touchable and we were chattering loudly and happily when my eldest cousin came in, still in his mujahit uniform. An enormous grin was spread over his face.

I was bursting with questions. "Did you kill the Greeks?" I blurted out.

He simply nodded his head and carried on smiling. To our delight, he then explained what had happened.

A handful of mujahits had gathered by the coffee bar in İpsillat, from which vantage point they could see the Greek army advancing in the far distance. The old single-firing rifles they'd been issued with were pretty near useless in that situation, our cousin went on, but the mujahits began to fire at will anyway. Then one of the Turkish Cypriot soldiers had a brilliant idea: why not set the fields alight to delay the Greek advance?

The mujahits set to their task immediately, setting fire to the crops, which were tinder-dry after weeks of the sun's unrelenting attention and were soon blazing fiercely. As luck would have it, the breeze was blowing in the right direction to help the mujahits' cause and within minutes a long, high, intimidating wall of fire was moving steadily towards the enemy. What's more, continued my cousin, the smoke being blown towards them was proving an effective screen and blocking off the Greeks' line of fire.

Within minutes of setting the fields alight, the mujahits heard the sound of fighter aircraft approaching from behind – but were they Turkish? No one could tell for sure at first, and the mujahits ran for cover. As they peered out from their hiding places, they saw the planes fly past them, past the wall of fire, and then – joy of joys – start to bombard the advancing Greek army.

"Turkey has come to save us!" cried the mujahits with one voice.

Incredulous, they watched the Greeks in the distance under bombardment and being stopped in their tracks. Surely, they thought, it would be a miracle if any of them escaped the merciless and seemingly relentless attacks of the Turkish air force. But within twenty minutes the attack had ceased and the fighter pilots flew their aircraft back towards the mujahits. Saluting their supporters with a celebratory rocking of their aircraft wings, they continued on a northward path. The mujahits, meanwhile, were jumping for joy, waving their rifles in the air and crying: "Yaşasın Türkler! (Long live the Turks!)"

Their joy transferred easily to those of us listening to our cousin's story. My brothers and I were whooping with delight and, in imitation of our mujahit friends, jumping up and down and firing imaginary guns at each other.

It wasn't long before my cousin had to leave the house to meet up again with his regiment. But within minutes of him leaving, my Granddad bustled into the house, followed by our other cousin, Mustafa. We noted with curiosity that he was carrying a polythene bag and making his way straight to the freezer.

"Ayşe," he called, addressing my nan, "I have brought some meat for you to cook." He placed the mysterious bag in the freezer compartment.

Nan was clearly confused. All the shops in the village had been closed because of the day's goings-on. "Where did you buy the meat?" she asked suspiciously.

"My friend İsmail," Granddad shouted back. Mustafa came up to me with a big grin spreading across his face and whispered into my ear: "Go and have a look at the meat."

Now it was my turn to be confused. "What for?" I asked. What on earth was so special about this meat that I should have to go and inspect it?

"Trust me, you will be shocked," Mustafa replied, his grin spreading even wider and his eyes glinting with mischief.

I walked slowly to the fridge/freezer and began to open the freezer door, then screamed in pain. I had forgotten to hold on to the cloth that was wrapped around the handle and had felt the excruciating jolt of the resultant electric shock.

Granddad heard my scream and told me, in no uncertain terms, to get away from the fridge/freezer immediately. "Don't touch the meat, it's for your nan," he ordered, and then proceeded to berate Mustafa for encouraging me to look in the freezer.

By now I was completely mystified. "What's the big deal?" I asked Mustafa.

His reply was chilling but went some way towards explaining his grin: "Granddad found the head of a Greek in the dried-out canal and he's playing a trick on Nan."

My brain struggled to comprehend what he was saying. Was he seriously telling me the freezer contained a man's severed head? The only reply I could come up with was: "You're lying, that's not nice!"

"Shh," he whispered, trying hard to suppress his mirth, "watch and wait."

So that's what I did, although I was barely able to contain my curiosity. We sat quietly in the living room and waited until, around fifteen minutes later, Nan removed the bag from the fridge and took it into the kitchen. Seconds later, the relative peace of the household was shattered by an eardrum-threatening scream.

Mustafa and Granddad's guffaws of satisfaction at the success of their prank were cut short as Nan appeared in the living room, brandishing a long rolling pin. "I'm gonna kill you," she screamed at Granddad, seasoning the threat with some carefully chosen oaths.

"How could you do that to me?" continued Nan, her screams turning to sobs. "Be, nedir bu kelle! (Oi, what is this head?)"

Granddad was still sniggering. "Wait until I see that İsmail," he spluttered, "he told me it was meat."

Nan was not to be fooled. "You're a liar!" she yelled. "Get it out of my house now, before I crack your skull!"

Granddad made his way carefully to the kitchen, ducking past Nan as she swung the rolling pin menacingly. He returned with the bag and walked towards the front door. He was still laughing as he opened the door. "I'll kill that İsmail," he insisted.

Nan swore at his retreating form, calling Granddad a prostitute of all things, then returned to the sanctuary of her kitchen. Mustafa carried on laughing, but the incident had left my brothers and I bewildered, confused as to how to react and not a little upset.

Later in life we found out that the bag contained nothing more than a pig's head, but the Muslim religion forbids the eating of pork. Mustafa, who was forever playing pranks on us, had the last laugh in making us think it was something more sinister.

The following day dawned bright, and we learned that my mother had arranged for her cousin Hasan to take us to Nicosia. Nan had advised her to go to the big city with us kids as, we were told, it would be much safer there. We had our breakfast – olives, bread, halloumi cheese and watermelon – then jumped into Hasan's camper van. As we set off for the capital, Nan observed Turkish tradition by throwing holy water at the van from behind. It's supposed to keep you safe on your journeys away from home.

CHAPTER NINE

Trench warfare

We went back to Nicosia to visit my mother's cousin's wife, Besime, and her son Ozzy. We soon found ourselves sitting, once again, on the raised pavement outside Ozzy's grandmother's house.

"What have you guys been up to?" asked Ozzy, impatient to hear our news. My brothers and I wasted no time in telling him all about our 'Great Escape', and he listened spellbound to the retelling of our adventures. But he had a tale of his own to tell: a couple of days before, hundreds of Turkish troops had parachuted into the fields at the end of his road. It was such a shame we had missed it, he said; it was an amazing sight.

"Have you seen any Turkish army tanks yet?" Ozzy asked. We shook our heads. "I've seen loads," he boasted, doing his best to equal the story of our exploits. "They've been travelling up and down the main road at the west end of our street. They're really huge things." Then, seeing our crestfallen expressions, he added: "Don't worry, it won't be long before another lot come by.

"Anyway, guess what? The paratroopers have dug some trenches in the fields down there." Ozzy waved an arm in the direction of the east end of his street. "They're not using them anymore, so me and my friends have started up our own armies. One army occupy the derelict house across the road," another waving arm indicated the house in question, "and the other army use the trenches as their base. Do you guys want to join in the fight?"

Did we? We didn't have to think too long. "OK," I replied, trying to force some nonchalance into my voice.

"Which camp do you want, the old house or the trenches?" asked Ozzy.

"We'll take the trenches," I said decisively.

"Oh well, that makes you guys my enemies then," explained Ozzy. "I'm with the gang in the old house. It doesn't matter though, it's only for fun. Do you guys have your own kuş lastik?"

Not for the first time on that holiday, I was nonplussed. "Er, no, what's that?" I asked.

He was referring to a catapult, used for shooting at birds and made from a long rubber band attached to a piece of leather in which stones were placed. "Give me some money and I'll get you guys one each," said Ozzy, thrusting out his hand. "It will only cost a couple of mils." These were the currency in use in Cyprus at the time.

I dug in my pocket, pulled out a few coins and handed them over. Ozzy scampered away to a friend's house, returning a few minutes later with three new catapults.

The Green Line

"There you go," said Ozzy, handing over our new weapons and launching into an impromptu training session. "This is how you use them." He grabbed the end of the kuş lastik in his left hand, pulled the rubber over the top of his thumb and loaded the leather with a nice fat, weighty stone. "Pinch the leather holder tight with the forefinger and thumb of your right hand, then pull it right back towards your shoulder. Close one eye and aim with the tip of your left thumb, then ... let go." The stone flew straight and true, and with tremendous velocity, towards the derelict house across the road.

"Wow." We kuş lastik novices were impressed as the missile thudded, with a pleasingly loud sound, into the mud and straw brick of the old house, throwing up a large cloud of dust.

"See, it's easy," boasted Ozzy casually. But the proud warrior had some words of caution: "You have your own weapon, but be careful when you're playing these war games. Don't aim at someone's face or shoot hard at your enemy."

Ozzy called one of his friends over and explained: "These guys have joined your army. Take them to your trenches and we'll come over later to attack you all." He ended with a whoop: "Let the battle begin!"

Niazy, Erden and I followed our new comrade to the trenches, and on arrival we were amazed at their size. The soldiers had dug them in no time at all, the boy explained, but the lads had made one or two improvements of their own devising. Two long planks running across the width of the trenches had several pieces of string attached, and they had been fashioned into sinister-looking nooses. "This is where we hang our prisoners," explained the boy helpfully.

As we clambered down into the main trench, other boys from the gang began to arrive and we all introduced ourselves to each other.

"They're planning to attack us," said one of the youthful combatants. "Let's go and surprise attack them first," suggested another. "Collect your ammunition and let's go!"

We all collected a few small stones for our catapults, climbed out of the trench and ran towards the enemy gang's old house headquarters. There must have been at least fifteen of us running up the road and screaming "ateş! (fire!)" Our words were followed by actions as we started stoning the guys on both levels of the derelict house. They in turn were waving a Turkish flag and firing enthusiastically back at us. What had been a peaceful street seconds before had changed into a full-blown war scene.

It wasn't long before adults started pouring out of their homes, shouting at us to stop, but we had been seized by a frenzy and carried on firing. It took the actions of one brave woman to bring the battle to an end. Ozzy's mother stormed into the derelict house and emerged a few seconds later, pulling an indignant Ozzy out by the ear.

"I told you not to misbehave!" The mother's angry words rang through a street that was otherwise now largely silent. Ozzy was wailing in pain and his face had turned as red as a ripe watermelon.

"Let me go, you're hurting me," he protested loudly. "I'm sorry mum, I'm sorry!" He was bent over almost double as he tried to escape his mother's vengeful grasp.

"You're sorry?" she spluttered. "How many times do I have to tell you to be good? I'll show you what sorry is!"

The boy-warriors started to disperse. Some got a slap around the head as they made their way home; others ran and dodged their parents in the hope that when they returned home later – much later – things would have calmed down a bit.

We three brothers were greeted at the house by the unwelcome sight of Mother standing with her hands on her hips. Mother with her hands on her hips was never a good sign. "What have you boys been up to?" she inquired.

We shuffled our feet and exchanged nervous glances. At last, Niazy spoke up: "We were just playing war games."

Mother controlled her anger enough to hiss: "Get inside now before you get the same treatment as Ozzy."

We trooped into the house and sat quiet as church mice. Ozzy was sitting opposite us with his head down, sobbing seemingly inconsolably, but when the adults weren't looking he would look up and flash us a smile. We smiled back and gave him the thumbs up. We approved of the fun we had had, however short-lived it may have been.

The following day saw us continuing to play together but a resumption of catapult hostilities was out of the question, although it was suggested by some of the lads. We were playing happily with our marbles when one of the older boys, who was called Cemal (pronounced Jemal), came over to Ozzy and handed him what we all recognised as a used bullet.

"I've done it for you, and I got told off by my dad," said Cemal, with more than a hint of pride in his voice.

"Thanks a lot, I owe you one," replied Ozzy. Cemal's father was an electrician and had welding tools. The boy had managed to add a metal link at the end of the bullet so it could be put on a neck chain and be worn as jewellery.

"Hatıra olsun (let it be for remembrance)," said Cemal.

I was impressed and a little jealous. "Will he do one for me?" I asked. Ozzy asked his friend if he would do a similar job for me and Cemal nodded instantly. "You will have to give him the bullet and he'll do it for you," replied Ozzy.

"But where do I get the bullet from?"

"They're everywhere," said Ozzy. "We can look in the fields – that's where I found mine."

Ozzy led us to where he had found his bullet and we started searching the area. There were plenty of empty used shells, which we pocketed, and then suddenly I spotted a used rifle bullet. My joy was unconfined. "Ozzy, I've found one, I've found one!" I yelled.

Ozzy examined the bullet with professional interest. "Let's take it to Cemal and he can do it for you today," he suggested.

When we got back to Ozzy's nan's house there was no sign of Cemal. We trooped round to his house, which was only a few doors down, but nobody was in. "They must have gone out somewhere," said Ozzy. "We'll come back later."

That afternoon, we continued to play and chat, putting to the backs of our minds the previous day's battle, but our innocent games were soon interrupted by the real thing – the distant sound of guns. Greeks and Turks, it seemed, were fighting at the other end of the field.

To our amazement, Turkish armoured tanks started to roll past, one after another, on the main road at the west end of the street we were on. Every single kid scampered off to the main road and started to cheer the Turkish army. These tanks were massive, like nothing we'd ever seen before, and as they passed at a fair old lick they made the ground shake beneath our feet and left their tracks in the hot tarmac.

Once the armoured squadron had passed we rushed back to the house, to find our parents starting to panic. We should get out of the area, some were saying; others were insisting that the Turkish army would fend off the Greeks and would not get anywhere near us. It was a tough decision, accompanied by much heated discussion, but it was eventually decided that we should stay put for now.

Later that afternoon, Turkish planes flew low over our heads towards the arid fields at the east end of our street. On reaching the end of the field, they gained height then began to dump their loads of bombs on the enemy. Then, to our surprise, they turned in wide circles, screamed back past us and unloaded more bombs about a mile west of where we were. The truth dawned: we were being attacked from both ends. The Greeks were trying to capture this part of Nicosia by closing in on two sides.

"Oh my God," cried my mother, "they're trying to trap us."

"It's OK auntie, don't worry," replied Ozzy. "The Turkish Phantoms will stop them."

For nearly an hour, the planes continued to circle, strafing their targets with gunfire and dropping bombs in both the east and the west. Every bomb released brought a cheer from us. Then, just as suddenly as they had arrived, the pilots turned their aircrafts' noses away and within seconds there was total silence. The entire street erupted with joyous celebration: the Turkish army had halted the Greek advance in no time at all. We were safe again.

That evening, just as my thoughts were turning from the extraordinary battle we had witnessed and towards my prized bullet, Cemal turned up outside the house. He was sporting an eye patch and a bandage round his head.

"What happened to you?" asked a stunned Ozzy.

"I was welding a loop on a bullet for a friend when it exploded in my face," replied Cemal ruefully, lifting his hand gingerly to the bandage. "My dad went mad and told me not to touch his tools any more."

Cemal's father turned up and started to explain to my mother and aunt what had happened. He had warned Cemal not to mess about with bullets, he said, because he knew some bullets as well as their cartridges contained gunpowder. He had warned him that it was highly dangerous, but had he listened? No, and now he would lose the sight in one eye because of his stupidity.

The Green Line

"I found a bullet but I guess you can't do it for me now," I whispered to Cemal.

But the lad was obviously not one to be put off by such a trivial accident. "Give it to me," he replied, smiling broadly. "I'm not scared. I'll do it when my dad isn't around – but don't tell anybody."

"Yeah, don't worry, Cemal will still do it for you, he's cool," Ozzy whispered, returning Cemal's grin.

By sleight of hand I transferred the bullet into Cemal's hand and he slipped it into his pocket. No one had noticed. Meanwhile, however, his father was still on the warpath. "I hope you've learned a lesson now," he threatened, wagging a menacing forefinger at him.

"Yes, Dad," replied a meek Cemal, no longer smiling and with his head bowed.

His father was only just warming up. "It's a shame you had to lose an eye to learn a lesson," he stormed. "Don't do it again or you'll end up totally blind!" Poor Cemal, he must have got a real ear-bashing all that week from family and friends.

Ear-bashing or no ear-bashing, I saw him the following morning as we were playing on the road. He came up and said, "Don't worry, I haven't done it yet but I will as soon as I get a chance."

I wasn't so sure he should go through with the plan. "It doesn't matter, Cemal. Maybe you should listen to your dad and not do it any more," I suggested.

But he was insistent. "I said I'll do it for you and that's that. I won't go back on my word. It will be a gift from me to you and something for you to remember this war by when you get back to London."

"Thanks, but be careful," I replied. "I will feel really bad if you get hurt again."

Cemal dismissed my fears. "Don't worry, I know what to do this time," he said, and the huge smile on his face went some way towards reassuring me he really knew what he was doing. "I've got to go, I'll see you later."

Ozzy had disappeared somewhere that afternoon playing with his gang. Just as Cemal was walking away, two boys from Ozzy's gang came up to Niazy and me and started to chat. What was London like, they wanted to know. Did we really like Cyprus? And did we want to see their new camp, which was somewhere in the fields?

We had nothing much else to do, so I gave our assent. Niazy and I found ourselves following the boys as they led the way across the dry field. We walked for at least ten minutes in the fierce afternoon heat.

I was starting to get a little worried. "This camp – where is it?" I asked.

"Nearly there," replied one of the boys. And sure enough, we soon came to a little hut made of corrugated steel sheets with a door and a cut-out window.

"Buyurunuz! (welcome!)" cried one of the boys. "Come on in." We followed the boys in and sat down. "What do you think of our new camp?" continued the boy.

"It's OK, but it's very small," I replied.

The other boy went to the door, closed it and stood by it. His friend reached into his pocket and pulled out a loaded catapult. "Esirsiniz! (You're prisoners)," he shouted in triumph, taking aim at us with the catapult. "We've tricked you and now you're our prisoners!"

Niazy was following this rather disturbing conversation with some difficulty as his Turkish wasn't very good. "What's he saying?" he asked. I explained in English what was going on.

"You're joking," laughed my brother. Apparently, he found the fact that we had fallen into the boys' trap hysterically funny.

But our captors were in no mood for jollity. "Why is he laughing?" demanded the boy with the catapult. "This is no joke. You are our prisoners and we'll kill you both if you don't obey us!"

I interpreted the boys' message for Niazy, whose laughter froze in mid-air. I felt it was time to stand up to these kids. "Our gang will come and find us, and then you'll be in big trouble," I blustered. "Let us go now!"

The boys exchanged confident glances. "No chance," said the boy at the door. "They'll never find you here. They don't even know about this secret camp of ours." Now it was their turn to laugh as the ease with which they had tricked us sank in.

"What are we gonna do?" asked Niazy, instantly offering one solution: "Let's push them and make a run for it."

"But they'll stone us if we run," I pointed out.

"What are you two talking about?" shouted the boy with the catapult. "No speaking in English. Talk in Turkish or stay quiet!"

"My brother said that he is thirsty," I lied. "Do you have any water? It's very hot in here."

"There's no water and you will both starve to death," retorted the boy at the door.

So Niazy and I sat quietly while our captors conversed in Turkish. After about twenty minutes in the sweltering heat of the hut, the boy with the catapult stood up and handed another catapult to his friend.

"We're going to give you a chance to get away," he announced. "When we open the door, run as fast as you can. We'll count to ten then start firing at you."

Although this offered the chance of freedom, it didn't strike me as fair. "What if we don't go?" I asked. "Then we'll stone you at close range, right here," was the answer.

I explained to Niazy what we had to do. "Run fast and straight for ten seconds then start running in zigzags," I counselled. "They won't get us if they don't know where to aim." Niazy agreed.

Catapult boy was angry again. "What are you two talking about? I told you, no English!" he screamed.

"I'm just explaining to my brother what you want us to do," I countered. "He doesn't know much Turkish."

This seemed to satisfy him. "OK, get out now!" he shouted, and then he started to count. Niazy and I set off at top speed in the direction we'd come, then began running in zigzags once the boys started firing stones. Success! Our zigzag plan worked and they didn't hit us once. Just as our pace was dropping we saw some of our friends at the trenches and called out for help. They came running and I recounted what had happened.

One of our comrades considered the situation briefly. "You both go back to camp and rest," he instructed. "We'll get those two brats. Charge!"

Six or seven volunteers followed him and Niazy and I sat down to watch our former kidnappers being hunted down. Running as fast as their legs could carry them, they were nevertheless fairly easy targets for our saviours' catapults. A resounding "ouch!" rang out every time a well-aimed stone struck home. We were helpless with laughter as the two boys took a real pasting before surrendering to our gang.

That afternoon, my mother told us she had managed to get in touch with my half-brother Üner, and that we were going to visit him at his house, on Yenice Sokak in Nicosia's Çağlayan district. We made our way there by taxi and I met Üner's wife and three children for the first time.

The two sons, Kurşat and Urungu, who were of similar age to my brothers and me, showed us around their home. They had a swing at the front of the house, so we spent most of the time playing out front and taking turns on the swing, while their baby sister, Aysun, sat with my mother and sister in-law, Ayşe. The boys – who were in fact our half-nephews – introduced us to crickets, showing us how to catch the insects by stealth, imprison them in cupped hands then shake them vigorously so that they made a noise.

We were engrossed in some game or other and getting to know each other better when a sudden burst of gunfire, coming from very close by, shattered our composure. We were becoming used to explosions and small arms fire, but this was truly shocking.

"Get inside boys, quickly, quickly!" screamed Ayşe from the front door. We scrambled in and she slammed the door shut, locking it before moving through to the back room. The gunfire was increasing in intensity, and there seemed to be return fire.

Ayşe was beside herself with anxiety. "My God! What are we going to do?" she sobbed. "Üner's not here yet and he's got the car!"

Mother did her best to be the calming influence the situation demanded. "Let's all stay in the kitchen, near the garden door, and wait for Üner," she urged. "He should be here soon."

Mother and Ayşe continued to talk while Kurşat and I went back into the living room. "Are you scared?" asked Kurşat.

"No," I replied scornfully. "Watch this." I picked up a toy rifle and crawled to the front door. "Bang, bang, drr-drr-drr!" I was imitating the sound of small arms fire – now very familiar to me – and pointing the rifle at the door window. Urungu and Niazy came in, realised what I was doing and started laughing uproariously. I turned to look back at them and treated them to my widest grin.

My cockiness met with a startling response. "No!" screamed Ayşe, running towards me. Frantically, she

The Green Line

pulled me backwards and yelled: "You might get killed if the soldiers see you lying there with a gun. They might think it's real."

Ayşe wasn't the only one shocked by my actions. I received a stinging slap from Mother, and Kurşat had his ear twisted by his mother for allowing me to do such a stupid thing.

We all sat quietly in the kitchen with our heads down, looking up and sniggering whenever the adults weren't looking. The gunfire was by now becoming louder and more frequent, but finally we heard Üner's voice coming from outside. "Are you all OK?" he called anxiously. "Leave everything and run to my car, quickly."

Üner was tall with dark, shoulder length hair and a thick moustache, and he wore large-lensed glasses in thick black frames. I had met him before twice during his visits to London, but then he had had short hair and no moustache. I guess he didn't want to upset Dad but was free to have his hair as long as he wanted in his homeland.

"Quickly, follow me to the car and get in", he ordered.

The door was flung open and we flew to the waiting light blue Rover and piled in. Üner stomped on the accelerator and we sped away from the fighting and towards the relative safety of Ozzy's nan's house. Once we were safely established under that roof, Üner drove off somewhere else – I know not where – with his family, and that was the last I saw of that family that year.

Ozzy's mother said we could stay as long as we liked, and that suited us boys just fine. Once again, we had an exciting story to recount to Ozzy. "You guys are so lucky," he complained when he'd heard our breathless account of the latest events. "You always end up where the fighting is."

Lucky? Really? "Yeah, but we've been really lucky to get out of it too," I replied thoughtfully. Ozzy considered this and nodded his agreement.

That night the street was peaceful, with no sounds of fighting. To pass the time and break the comparative boredom, we played tag and hide and seek. Life was almost normal.

CHAPTER TEN

What is it like to be dead?

The following morning dawned, as usual, bright. I gobbled my breakfast eagerly then went outside to sit on the pavement in the growing heat. After a few minutes, Hasan drew up in his Volkswagen camper van, and parked up. "Hello Küfi," he called, leaning out of the window. "Where's your mother?"

I told him she was inside and he asked me to go and fetch her. I did as I was bidden and Mother followed me down the stairs. "Hello Hasan," she said. "What are you doing here?"

It turned out that Hasan had some good news. "I've heard the road to Famagusta is clear," he reported. "You can get a ship from there to Turkey, then make your way back to London by plane."

But Mother wasn't entirely convinced of the safety of the proposed journey. "How do you know the road is clear?" she asked.

"Friends told me, and some Turkish soldiers confirmed that they've taken over the area," said Hasan. He was starting to get impatient. "If you want me to take you, hurry up and get ready."

My mother's mind seemed made up, and she ran back up the stairs to gather our belongings. She wondered whether Ozzy and his mother would like to join us, but Ozzy's mother said she had registered with the British Consulate and was waiting to be evacuated.

"Are you sure you don't want to join us?" Mother asked her cousin.

"No, really, we were told to wait and they would contact us when they were ready to evacuate us," she insisted. "You go and don't worry about us. We'll be fine." She enveloped my mother in a loving embrace.

Hasan helped us to load his camper van and we all climbed aboard. As we set off for Famagusta, along the street where we'd had so many adventures, we waved goodbye to Ozzy and his friends. We couldn't help wondering if we would see them again.

Hasan seemed excited about our prospects. "This time tomorrow you boys will be back in London," he called over his shoulder. There was only one fitting response from us boys: "Yippee!"

Sitting at the back of the camper van, we played cards on the table to pass the time. We chattered non-stop about our adventures and laughed happily at some of the naughty things we'd got up to during that extraordinary holiday. For the first time in a long while, Mother looked relaxed and was wearing a big smile. It seemed she had found it in her heart

The Green Line

to forgive Hasan for leaving us behind when there were problems in İpsillat.

In about half an hour we reached a village called Çatoz, which has now been renamed Serdarlı. Mother's smile froze on her face. The houses in the village were in flames.

"Boys, put your hands over your ears, quickly!" shouted Hasan as he drove past the burning houses. I was horrified but I didn't obey his instructions and as we passed one of the houses I could hear the terrible sound of people screaming inside.

"What happened here?" cried mother in desperation, looking at Hasan for an answer. But how could he know? He had no reply to give apart from a shrug of his shoulders.

"I thought you said it was going to be safe," continued Mother. "What on earth is happening?"

"I really don't know," said Hasan. An unlikely possibility occurred to him. "Maybe they were Greeks captured by Turkish soldiers." He was hoping this was the case, otherwise we were definitely in dangerous territory.

Mother was horrified at the plight of these poor people, no matter what nationality they were, trapped inside houses that had been set alight deliberately.

"Can't we stop to help them?" she asked desperately.

"I don't know what to do," replied Hasan, continuing to drive past this tragedy in the making.

"But these people are being burnt alive!" cried Mother.

"Oh no! Oh no! They are Greek soldiers," Hasan shouted.

At that moment, things took a turn for the worse. In front of us, in the distance, we made out the unmistakable shapes of Greek soldiers – and we were heading straight towards them.

This was too much for Mother. "Turn the van back, quick!" she urged.

Hasan was distraught. "I can't," he protested. "The road's too narrow and if we turn they'll just open fire on us." An idea occurred to him, and he took his eyes off the road, turned to me and, looking me straight in the eye, started speaking urgently. "Küfi, I want you to do me a favour and start to cry."

Of all the strange things that had happened to me since my arrival in Cyprus, this request struck me as among the weirdest. "Why?" I asked.

"If they see you crying they may feel sorry for you and let us go," Hasan explained. "Just pretend to be scared."

"I'm not scared and I'm not going to cry." I replied. We were now getting very near the soldiers.

Seeing he was getting nowhere with me, Hasan changed tack and started pleading with Niazy. "You do it son, please cry."

Niazy was not to be persuaded. "No, I'm not scared either," he maintained. By now, we were almost upon the soldiers and Hasan was screaming. "What the fuck's wrong with your children?" he demanded of Mother. "Tell them to fucking cry or we'll all die!"

Mother laughed nervously. "I can't make them cry if they're not afraid," she responded.

"Erden, cry now! I want you to cry now!" yelled Hasan to my five-year-old brother.

"Go on Erden, do as he says," prompted my mother.

But Erden was reluctant too. "No, I'm not scared either. Why should I cry if the others won't cry?" he asked.

Hasan's response was shocking. He half-turned, put his left arm over the back of his seat, grabbed some flesh from Erden's leg and pinched with all his might. Sure enough, Erden began to wail like a crazy kid, floods of tears pouring from his eyes.

"So you boys won't cry, huh?" Hasan pulled up beside one of the Greek soldiers, who had halted him with a hand gesture. "Why is the boy crying?" he demanded in Greek.

My mother and Hasan understood and were able to communicate in Greek as they had both learned the language in their childhood. "Oh, the little boy's scared, that's why he's crying," replied Hasan casually.

The soldier's face had turned scarlet with anger. He levelled his machine gun and pointed it through the driver's window at us three boys in the back. "Tell him to stop crying right now or I'll kill you all!" he shouted. Hasan panicked and turned round to Erden.

"You must stop crying now or this man is going to kill all of us," he said, stroking Erden's arm gently to calm him. "Stop crying. Stop crying, please, please, please stop crying." He turned to Mother. "Tell your son to stop crying, you heard what the man said!"

"Erden, stop crying, darling." Mother's tone was soothing. "I know what he did wasn't nice." Erden gritted his teeth tightly and stopped crying out loud, but you could see he was still in pain and really wanted to lash out.

"I want you all to get out of the van," ordered the soldier. Mother told us to get out slowly, keep still and do whatever she would ask of us. When we had all climbed down, the soldier pointed to a pile of pebbledash stone and told us boys to sit on it.

My mother and Hasan started to explain that we were tourists and were trying to get back home to London. The soldier reminded them that they were still Turkish even though they no longer lived in Cyprus.

Mother stood up bravely to the gun-wielding tough. "You can do whatever you like to me or Hasan, but you can't touch the children," she pointed out proudly. "They were born in England and have British passports. If the British government finds out they've gone missing or have been killed, your country will be in deep trouble. Where is your superior? I want to speak to your superior."

The soldier ordered one of his men to call their superior officer. He came quite quickly and listened carefully to Mother's explanation of the situation. Hasan, however, was taken away to an empty house to be interrogated. We watched horror-struck as he was marched away.

Mother continued to ramble on, and the officer told her to be quiet, adding that he would cut her throat. To emphasise the threat, he made the familiar gesture with a finger running across his throat.

Niazy, Erden and I knew not what was being said as the adults were all talking in Greek, but we did know Mum was afraid. Her face had turned bright red, and we had never seen her like that before.

Mother responded with the same action, running her finger across her throat and saying: "You can cut my throat if you like but you can't lay a finger on my kids." The officer laughed at her bravery.

Things suddenly took a turn for the better in a quite unexpected fashion. "Can you make Greek coffee?" the officer asked my mother.

"Of course I can," replied mother.

The officer smiled encouragingly. "OK, if you make coffee for me and my men, I will let you all go," he said.

This was amazing. Were we to be saved by our mother's skill with hot water and coffee?

We were to make no effort to run away, Mother told us sternly; we were, after all, surrounded by minefields and the soldiers were keeping a watchful eye on us. She was going to make some coffee for the soldiers, she explained, but she would return soon. We nodded: we understood her instructions.

"Don't do anything silly, just keep still and wait for me," she added, then she disappeared behind us with the officer and another soldier.

We sat quietly on the pile of stones, Erden in the middle, to the left of me, and Niazy next to him. This was it, I thought. This really was the end for us. I looked over at the young soldier who was pointing his rifle at us and saw with a shock that he was shaking like a leaf.

Later in life I realised that he did not want us to make a run for it as it would have been his duty to shoot us down, and that was a situation he did not want to be put in. That explained why he was shaking so violently. I turned around and looked at him boldly several times and his nervous tremor never relaxed for one moment.

The other soldiers had disappeared with Mum and Hasan. Were they going to be shot? I looked down at the pile of stones and picked up one. It was so large that I couldn't wrap my fingers all the way round it. As our guard eyed me anxiously, I pondered: Should I try to throw this stone into his face and make a run for it with the boys? No, I decided, we should wait. Running would mean certain death. Nevertheless, I kept the stone close beside me in case I heard the gunshots that would tell me Mum and Hasan had been slaughtered.

Meanwhile, dismal thoughts similar to mine were running through my brothers' minds. "We're going to die, aren't we?" sniffed Niazy, his chin beginning to wobble.

It was up to me to be positive and rally my brothers. "No, it's going to be all right," I assured Niazy and Erden. "They'll let us go after Mum has made them coffee. Just stay calm and don't worry about a thing."

I needed to get their minds occupied with something other than our plight, I decided. There were few resources available to me, but an idea occurred and I turned to my brothers.

"OK, see these stones we're sitting on? Let's see who can make the biggest pile between our legs. The one with the biggest pile is the winner." They sighed and listlessly started picking up stones, filling the gaps between their crossed legs, and I slowly began to join in.

My mind was certainly not on the game; it was on what was about to happen to us. I was not afraid, but I was worried for my mother and brothers. What were they doing with Mum? Did they really only want her to make them coffee or were they going to rape and beat her before the kill? What about Hasan? Was he being tortured while we sat out here in the sun awaiting our death?

I accepted this was going to be the end of life for us, but I hoped the end would be fast and painless. And I felt so helpless, gutted that our lives were going to end up being so short, especially on our first ever holiday. What was all that about?

What would it be like to be dead, I wondered, picking up another stone. Would we be in total darkness? Well, I guessed we were soon going to find out.

Niazy paused in his game, a stone poised in his hand. "Why are we playing games?" he asked. "They're going to kill us, aren't they?"

"Is that true?" put in Erden anxiously. "Are we going to be shot?"

My reply was calm and firm despite my true feelings. "No, everything will be OK. Mum will be back soon, you just wait and see."

"I hope so," replied Erden. He resumed the game on his own, which made him the winner.

"I won!", he cried out joyously, forgetting about our perilous situation we were in. Me, I was thinking that it was a miracle he hadn't hurt himself with those stones.

Once more I looked over at the soldier guarding us, then at the large stone I had put aside. Should I? If we were going to die, we might as well die fighting. Again, cool reason rose to the surface of my thoughts. No, just wait, I told myself. Let's see what happens.

Although I was trying to distract my brother's attention, I felt Niazy was thinking along the same lines. He looked me straight in the eye, showed me a large stone he was holding and discreetly pointed to the kuş lastik that was poking out of his pocket, then glanced over to the soldier. I shook my head at him, and hoped he would not try anything drastic without my consent.

At that moment, Hasan returned with one of the soldiers, looking a little shaken. "Where's your mummy?" he asked, looking intently at me with glazed eyes.

"She went to make coffee for the soldiers, somewhere behind us," I explained.

"Stay calm and don't do anything silly," Hasan replied.

Mother had been gone nearly forty minutes now, and my mind started to go into overdrive with a thousand speculations.

If they were going to kill us, how were they going to do it? Shoot us in the head or in the body? What if they did to us what they had done to those villagers: tie us up and lock us in one of the houses before setting it alight? Being burned alive wasn't top of my list of ways to die. Why

The Green Line

didn't Hasan try to fight one of the soldiers, take his gun and save us all?

I kept my eye continually on Hasan in case he did try something. If he did, I could surely help and get my brothers away. But my hopes were in vain and we all sat quietly, waiting for something – anything – to happen.

At last, Mother appeared with the officer with whom she had gone away. To our astonishment, he was smiling and chatting away to her in Greek. Evidently, Mother's coffee had done the trick. "Keep still boys, we'll be going soon!" she said cheerfully, walking towards the van.

"OK, you can all go," said the officer, and Hasan told us to get a move on and jump in his van ready for the off.

Mother was still concerned. "What if we get stopped by other Greek soldiers?" she asked the officer. "We'll have a problem again, won't we?" An idea occurred to her. "Please, can you write a little note saying you've set us free and we're to be given free passage?"

The officer agreed it was a reasonable idea and, pulling a piece of paper from his pocket, started jotting down a message in Greek. "Thank you," said mother, taking the note eagerly from his hand.

As I followed my brothers into the back of the camper van, who should be standing by the door but the Greek soldier who had threatened to shoot us all if Erden did not stop crying. He reached out and stroked my face with his dirty hands.

"Güzel çocuk (nice child)," he said in broken Turkish, smiling as I scrambled up into the van. I cringed but smiled back as he closed the camper's side door behind me.

Mother and Hasan got into the van, saying goodbye to the soldiers and thanking them profusely. Hasan started the engine and turned the camper van round to face the direction we had come. He drove away slowly, asking us to wave goodbye to the nice soldiers – and for once we did as he asked.

Now we were all free of a troubling experience, emotion began to shake Mother. "I can't believe they let us go," she sobbed, tears starting from her eyes.

But Hasan was not so sure we were safe. "It could be a trick," he muttered bitterly. "They could open fire at us or blow the van up before we have a chance to get away." He thought for a moment. "Boys, I want you all to keep your heads down just in case."

We had gone no further than a hundred and fifty metres down the road before we were waved down by another Greek soldier brandishing a gun. Hasan had no choice other than to pull up beside him. A few words in Greek were exchanged between the two, then Hasan handed the officer's note to the soldier. We waited anxiously as he took in the contents. What exactly had been written?

The soldier read the note, shrugged, gave it back to Hasan and waved him on. Apparently our officer had been as good as his word.

Hasan drove on again, past the smouldering ruins of the houses from where we had heard those terrible cries a little while before. This time there were no screams. The inhabitants were dead.

As we began to exit the village, Hasan put his foot down and the camper van hurtled down the road. "I can't believe it! I can't believe we've come out of this alive!" cried Hasan, with sweat pouring down his forehead. Mother echoed his relief by repeatedly thanking God for our delivery from peril.

Hasan now demanded to know what had happened while Mother was with the soldiers, out of our view. "What did they do to you?" he asked.

It was mother's turn to shrug. "Nothing," she said. "I just made them some coffee. They took me to an empty house but the door was locked. They were going to shoot the lock but I stopped them. If my children heard gunshots they might have got the wrong idea and panicked, I told them. So they just kicked the door down. I went into the kitchen, found some coffee and made some for them. They sat down and drank it, and that was that."

Now Mother wanted to know what had happened to Hasan. We listened intently as he told his tale.

"They took me to a house and questioned me. I showed them my British passport and said I was only here on holiday, but they insisted I was still Turkish even if I had a British passport. So I told them the kids were totally innocent and should be set free, and they would need me to drive them back."

Hasan's incredulity at our escape surfaced again. "I can't bloody believe our luck," he yelled triumphantly. "How on earth did we survive that ordeal?"

Mother's emotion had by now turned from relief to anger. "How on earth did you get us into that ordeal in the first place?" she hissed. "You assured me it would be safe!"

"How was I to know they'd taken over the village?" spluttered Hasan. "Just thank God we've come out of this alive."

Mother turned to us three boys and asked if we were all right. We nodded, and I told her what we had been doing while she was making the coffee.

Mother's thoughts turned to the poor inhabitants of the burned village, and the tears started to flow again. "The whole village has been massacred," she wailed. "Those poor women and children were burned alive. We must inform the Turkish authorities when we get back to Nicosia." Hasan agreed and replied that we would do just that.

We were far from safety when, after an uneventful journey, we arrived back in Nicosia. The sights and sounds of battle were filling the air, and we were stopped by a Turkish soldier. Hasan explained what had happened to us.

The soldier didn't seem to believe our story. "How did you get out of there alive?" he asked, incredulous.

"We just did," answered Hasan. "Only God knows how. Just direct us to the Turkish authorities so we can tell them where we were captured. They need to know before the Greeks advance and massacre more of our people."

Battle was still raging and bullets were zipping all over the place. A nearby square was the scene of particularly fierce fighting. "It's too dangerous for you to see anybody now," replied the soldier.

But Mother was not to be put off by a few bullets: "Every second counts. We must see someone immediately," she insisted.

The soldier thought for a moment, then relented with a sigh. "OK, OK, follow me," he instructed. "Tell the kids to keep their heads down and to run as fast as they can." We jumped out of the van and the soldier pointed in the direction he wanted us to run. "Follow me, and keep your heads down!" he repeated.

We began to run, half bent over. We were caught in the middle of vicious crossfire, and could hear the occasional bullet sing past our ears, but somehow we made it to the other side of the square. Another narrow escape.

We entered a building and the soldier explained to an official that we had vital information, then left to return to the fighting.

We were ushered into a room and Hasan and Mother recounted our ordeal to two government officials. They listened with obvious disbelief. "Why on earth would they set you free?" asked one.

"Because we had British passports," replied Mother.

"But that hasn't stopped them killing other people," the official pointed out. "British Turks have lost their lives. Their passports didn't save them."

Mother turned to Hasan with a look of horror. "Now they think we're spies," she said. She turned back to the official. "Will you just listen to what I'm saying and forget about us getting away alive?" she pleaded. "The Greeks have taken over Çatoz village and have killed everyone who lived there. They will move on and take over another village if you don't put a stop to it immediately."

It later dawned on me that my grandparents' village of İpsillat was not far from where we had been captured. This was why Mother was so concerned; she was worried that the Greeks would reach İpsillat and kill her parents.

The official would not be contradicted. "We secured that area yesterday and we have a hold on it," he replied firmly.

"Not any more, I can assure you of that," said Mother. "We're wasting time. Please call someone to do something now before it's too late."

"OK, I'll see what I can do." The official was calm but the look of disbelief on his face was plain to see. He left the room, but not before positioning a soldier by the door. Meanwhile, Hasan had been taken to another room to be questioned separately.

I was confused by these latest events. "What's the matter, Mummy?" I asked.

"It seems they don't believe our story," said Mother angrily. "They think we're spies." Our extraordinary story had taken one incredible twist too many, it seemed.

We were left, fuming, in the room for a good twenty minutes before the official returned. "I've called one of the generals of the Turkish army to send some fighter planes to check out your story," he told us. "He has also confirmed that we secured that area yesterday."

Mother was satisfied. "Good, then it won't be long before you realise we are telling you the truth." We settled down to await the outcome of the pilots' mission.

An hour or more passed, and gradually the shooting outside calmed down. Then the door opened and one of the official's staff hurried in with a piece of paper in his hand. The official read slowly and, at last, turned to us.

"Well done," he said, with a touch of embarrassment. "Thank you for passing on this information; you may have saved many lives. The fighter pilots have flown out to that area and are now attacking the enemy. We don't know how the Greeks managed to get past our lines of defence." A big grin spread across his face.

Relief billowed out across the room like a wave, and Mother, too, began to smile. The whole story of our ordeal began to spill out of her. She told the official how brave her children were and that we had refused to cry because we were not afraid. He turned to me, and he was smiling.

"We need men like you," he beamed at me. "If I get you a uniform and a gun, will you join the Turkish army and help kill these Greeks?" I looked at my mother but, in my shyness, did not reply.

"What do you say?" asked the official again. I shrugged my shoulders. He smiled again, patted my head and left the room.

I was curious to know whether he had meant what he said, and asked Mother. "Why? Would you take up the offer and stay even if I went back to London?" she asked in turn.

I allowed myself a little grin and swagger. "If they really gave me a real gun. Wow, that would be so cool!"

Mum grinned too. "No, he was only joking with you," she confirmed.

I blushed. I felt a real fool for falling for what that stupid official had said. Why had he joked like that and built my hopes up? My imagination started to create pictures and I visualised myself in uniform, holding a machine gun and fighting off the enemy. Then the door opened, the official returned and my heroic vision vanished.

To my further embarrassment, Mother explained to the official that I was ready and willing to take him up on his offer. He laughed long and loud and, patting me on the head again, cried: "Aslansin (you're a lion)! I'll sort you out a uniform immediately."

I turned to my mother. "Is it true? But you said he was joking," I complained, but Mother merely burst into laughter. I was totally lost in confusion at adults' weird ways, and turned away to try to puzzle it out.

The Green Line

Meanwhile, the official had some good news. "It's safe for you to leave now," he smiled. "The fighting outside has stopped. Thank you so much for telling us about the Greek soldiers taking over that area. We've been able to secure it again." He led us out of the building and waved goodbye as we climbed into Hasan's van.

As we drove to Mother's cousin Feriha's house, I reflected on our latest adventures. I couldn't help feeling sorry for the Greek soldiers who had let us go free – especially the officer who had made the decision. I hoped that he was not harmed and had managed to keep out of the way of the Turkish air force. I guess I will never know.

Did we do the right thing by informing of the Greeks' whereabouts? They did spare our lives, true, but they also burned those poor people alive in their houses.

I was still musing anxiously when we arrived at cousin Feriha's house, in the Marmara district on the outskirts of Nicosia. She offered us cold drinks and the adults sat down and had some well-earned coffee. Feriha asked her son to show us three boys something he had made, and we followed him outside to a garden shed.

"Aha bak (Here, look)," he said, handing me a makeshift, hand-made rifle. It consisted of a long piece of wood for the barrel, split at one end and nailed to a triangular piece of wood that formed the butt. Attached to the butt end by a black rubber band was a clothes peg and at the front of the barrel was a long, dangling chain of rubber bands.

I was fascinated and couldn't help thinking back to the official who had offered me a gun – a real gun – of my own. Or so I had thought. Dismissing this thought, I watched as the boy took his rifle from me to demonstrate how it worked.

He pulled the chain of bands tight and secured it in the clothes peg. Picking up a stone, he placed it in front of the peg between one of the chained bands, hoisted the gun to his shoulder and aimed at a tree, then pressed down on the peg with his thumb to release the taught string of rubber bands. The stone whizzed away at tremendous speed and hit the tree with an audible crack.

My brothers and I gasped. "Can we make one for ourselves?" I asked.

"Yes, of course," replied the boy. "I'll show you how."

Scrabbling among the scraps of old wood that littered the shed, he found us some useful pieces, gave each of us a peg from his mother's washing line and then started to cut narrow strips from an old bicycle inner tube, which were to act as rubber bands. He showed us how to tie the black rubber bands together to create a long string that acted like a catapult once it was stretched back to the peg.

The time flew by as we immersed ourselves in the task. We were getting on so well and were so busy in our arms manufacture that Feriha asked us to stay the night. Hasan had left a long while before, while we boys were busy in the shed.

The following afternoon we made our way to Ozzy's nan's house by bus. The three of us leapt off the bus and swaggered down the road, side by side with our rifles strapped over our shoulders. We fancied we looked just like daredevil cowboys in a Western film.

Ozzy saw us coming. "Cor," he cried, "they look cool!" We showed him how our primitive rifles worked, then sat down on our usual spot on the pavement and started to relate our incredible tale.

Ozzy was suitably impressed. "Wow, you guys are getting all the adventures," he observed, "but you were really lucky to come out alive."

We sat there on the pavement until the sun went down. We had our listener enthralled and we didn't want to miss out a single detail.

CHAPTER ELEVEN

Pure torture

In the days that followed, we became aware that the fighting had calmed down. We spent each long, hot day playing with Ozzy and the local boys in the fields, using our wooden rifles and collecting used and live bullets and bits of bomb shrapnel. Little did we know that messing around with the shrapnel would later affect our health.

One day I came across Cemal again. As he came up to me, he was smiling as usual. "Here you go," he said, passing over the bullet I had given him so he could add a loop to it.

I was overcome. "Wow, thanks Cemal," I stammered. "I didn't think you would do this for me."

"Hatıra olsun (let it be for remembrance). A promise is a promise, but," Cemal paused and glanced around, then looked me sternly in the eye, "don't you dare tell anybody I did this for you."

I assured him that our secret was safe and he turned to walk away. Just then, one of the local lads started running towards us. "Hey, did you hear what happened to one of our friends?" he shouted. Breathlessly, he explained that

The Green Line

some Turkish tanks, returning from battle, had come to a halt at one end of a field where they had been met by excited, cheering crowds.

"My friend climbed on to one of the tanks," the boy went on. "All he had on were his shorts and flip flops, no top. He tried to show off by lying down on the front of the tank, but he immediately began to scream and jumped off. His back was burnt and the skin was peeling off. Either the tank had got so hot from enemy bombs or the scorching sun had heated the metal. Anyway, the boy's back and legs were burnt and they took him straight off to hospital."

"So don't try anything like that when we see a tank," I warned my brothers. As I spoke, trucks filled with Turkish soldiers started to pass by at the east end of the road, where the fields started. Naturally, we all scampered towards them. There must have been fifteen trucks, each carrying at least twenty soldiers. They all looked so young – around sixteen to eighteen years old – tired and drained from the punishing heat.

"Are you hungry, my son?" cried out a woman to one of the soldiers.

"No Auntie, God bless you, but we are thirsty," he replied. All the women and children turned and ran into their homes, returning seconds later laden with bread and water. There was a mad rush to hand these out to the soldiers as their trucks moved slowly past.

"Thank you for saving us, and may God keep you safe," called the women as they rushed in and out of their houses, carrying water to as many soldiers as they could.

"Yaşasın Türkler! (Long live the Turkish!)," the children cried out as they waved at the soldiers who were being transported into battle.

The trucks moved on slowly with the refreshed soldiers waving in turn to us. What on earth was going through their minds, I wondered.

But there was something else on my mind, and it was troubling me. Over the previous week or so, my brothers and I had started to developed scabs on our arms and legs. Mother had told us not to play with bomb shrapnel but now the chemicals on those jagged pieces of broken metal had infected our skin, and the scabs were spreading fast. To Mother's dismay, the hospitals were too busy with the casualties of war to deal with trifling matters such as these.

Mother drew me aside one day. "Küfi, we need to treat these scabs," she said. "Otherwise they will spread all over your body fast." I agreed some treatment was necessary but wondered how she was going to do it.

"The locals say the best way is to soak a tea towel in boiling water, put the towel over the scab and then pull it off quickly," said Mother. "The scab comes away with the towel. It will hurt a bit but we must do something now. We'll do your scabs first and you must try to be brave and not cry, or Niazy and Erden won't let us do it for them."

I didn't like the sound of this treatment one little bit. "Maybe the scabs will go away by themselves if we leave them," I suggested hopefully.

The Green Line

Mother had been expecting this suggestion. "No, they won't, and they will spread everywhere on your body if we don't do something now," she insisted.

I sighed and resigned myself to some pain. Hadn't I already shown extraordinary bravery many times during this incredible holiday? What was a little pain compared to the terror we had experienced? "OK, I'll let you do it," I replied.

Mother called Niazy and Erden to join us on the stairs outside the house. She explained to my brothers what was going to happen. The women, who had already been boiling water in a metal bucket, brought clean tea towels to Mother. Ozzy's nan then carried the bucket of boiling water over to us. I sat on the steps, held out my left arm, gritted my teeth and looked the other way.

I felt the scalding hot cloth cover my arm, and screamed with pain as Ozzy's nan pulled the scabs off my arm. She went on to treat my other arm and both legs, and each time I couldn't help but scream; it was indescribably painful. Eventually, after what seemed like weeks of torture, it was all over and my tanned skin no longer had scabs but raw patches of pink flesh, which had to be wiped again with a hot cloth to ensure no germs were left behind.

Now it was my brothers' turn. They tried to get away but the front door was blocked by women. Niazy screamed blue murder as they held him down and ripped his scabs away, then Erden had his turn. It hurt me just as much to watch them in such pain as the process had hurt me.

But that wasn't the end of our ordeal. Oh no. Those damned scabs kept on reappearing and we had to go through the whole agonising process again at least two more times in the following weeks. But we eventually got used to the idea and were able to accept the pain much more readily than when we had first experienced it. We still screamed, mind you, but not as loudly, and tears did not follow.

One day it was announced that the Turkish army had captured hundreds of Greek prisoners and were going to transport them in coaches on the main road, past our street. "Please do not throw stones at the coaches," pleaded a man with a megaphone. "They are borrowed vehicles and we do not want them damaged."

To be honest, it would probably have been better if we had not been informed of what was going to happen. Every single kid and adult made their way to the main road to watch. We waited for what seemed like hours, then a parade of Turkish soldiers in jeeps passed by, met by thunderous cheers.

Then came the coaches – at least seven of them – with the prisoners. Their hands were tied and they were blindfolded. Rage engulfed the crowd and the coaches were met by a barrage of booing, swearing and shaking fists. Soon, worse followed.

We kids picked up stones and hurled them at the coach windows in the hope that we would hit a prisoner. This was war, and we had grown accustomed to it. One of our comrades threw a particularly large missile, which smashed through the glass and hit a prisoner on the side of the head. Blood started from the blindfolded man's head and cheers rang out from the crowd.

At the time, our comrade was ecstatic with the result of his shot, jumping up and down and yelling, "I got one of them", but later he felt sorry for what he had done. Well, we were in the middle of a war, and all the feelings that war brings out in the human animal had risen in us too.

We were angry; hatred had been stirred up inside us. At the same time, a great feeling of patriotism was welling to the surface: we were Turkish and damned proud of it. Nobody had the right to massacre our people or take our land away from us.

Cyprus had been the home of my father, mother, grandparents and ancestors. Cyprus was ours as much as it was anyone else's. Even though we had never before left the United Kingdom and this was our first visit to the island, we considered it our homeland and nobody was going to take it away from us.

CHAPTER TWELVE

Thoughts of home

A couple of days passed – days in which we continued to play in the fields and wonder when, if ever, we would see our London home again. During our games we started to see soldiers wearing unfamiliar light blue berets; they belonged to a United Nations force that was trying to uphold a fragile peace.

After all the fighting, a ceasefire had been declared. By that time, the Turkish army had managed to occupy the northern third of the island. We were separated from the Greeks by a no man's land that ran from east to west, guarded by both sides and occupied by UN peacekeeping forces.

So things were happening on the political front ... and there were new developments on a personal level, too. Mother woke us one morning and told us we would finally be going home.

All foreign women and children still in Cyprus had been told, she explained, to meet up at a specific location in Nicosia. From there we would be evacuated to the

British army base in Akrotiri, then flown back to London. The truth took a little time to sink in ... at last, after all our trials, we were going home.

We dressed hurriedly, wolfed down some food and ran to catch a coach with Ozzy and his mother to the meeting point. On arrival at midday, we found ourselves in a strange situation. Hundreds of women and children were lined up in queues, waiting for UN soldiers to arrange our evacuation.

We had long since become accustomed to setbacks in our efforts to avoid trouble, and it wasn't long before we found that, as usual, there was a problem this time too. The area between us and the coaches that were to take us to either Akrotiri or Dhekelia had been occupied by Greek soldiers, we found. In order to get to the coaches we would have to walk through a zone occupied by our enemies.

A UN soldier walked towards us from the barriers and explained that we would not be able to board the coaches that day. Everybody should return to their hotels, he recommended. Hotels? What hotels?

Some women started to protest loudly: they hadn't come all this way for nothing, they said; the UN force should do something to ensure we got to the coaches. But it wasn't safe, the soldiers insisted, and by no means should we attempt to pass through. This wasn't good enough for one woman, who said she wasn't afraid and made her way to the barrier, calling on others to join her.

Ozzy's mum held an urgent consultation with mine, who agreed that we should take a chance: we had to try to get that coach to the British base. This was the best chance we'd had to get away from the dangers that had racked the island, and it would be a crying shame to lose it. Our minds were made up.

Ozzy's mum walked ahead of the rest of us and queued up behind some women and children who had already formed a lengthy line. We stood behind Ozzy and waited for the instruction to proceed. One of the UN soldiers was examining the Greek-occupied zone intently through a pair of binoculars.

Another blue-bereted soldier, standing by the barriers at the front of the queue, turned to address us: "OK, I can't stop you if you are determined to go, but I want you to listen very carefully to what I tell you.

"Walk very slowly and keep your arms by your sides. If we spot any suspicious moves by the Greek soldiers, we will call you to come back as quickly as you can. And please make sure you do."

"Let's go, girls," cried the woman at the front, and she set out past the UN barrier. We all followed behind, doing as the soldier had instructed. Mum was holding on to Niazy's and Erden's hands as I walked ahead of them.

When we had cleared about thirty feet, I looked up at the apartment block ahead on our right, to see if I could see any Greek soldiers. After about another twenty feet, I spotted some soldiers on a balcony. They were standing in silence, watching us shuffling forward. We were getting close to the coaches now. We had covered another twenty feet when an urgent voice rang out from behind us.

The Green Line

"Come back! Come back!" The urgent tone in the UN man's voice was unmistakeable and we didn't need to be told twice. The orderly line dissolved in panic and everyone, women and children, ran back to the safety of the barriers, covering their heads in terror.

Everyone, that is, except us.

"Why is he calling us back, Mum?" I asked. "We were nearly there."

"I don't know," replied Mother. "We'd better go back."

I looked around and saw that the four of us – Mother, Niazy, Erden and I – were standing perfectly alone. We had been deserted in the panicked rush back to the barriers. I looked up at the apartment block and made out the figure of one of the soldiers. He was pointing his rifle at us. My attention was then caught by another soldier who was waving to us, urging us to carry on. What to do?

"Geliniz Geri! Ates edecekler (Come back! They are going to shoot)," cried some of the women hysterically from the safety of the barriers.

"Come on Küfi, let's go back, best not take any chances," said Mum. She turned around, still holding on to Niazy's and Erden's hands. I turned and trudged back with them. I couldn't believe we had been so close to boarding that coach home, and felt bitterly disappointed.

The UN soldier who had addressed us just a couple of minutes earlier was apologetic but, he explained, he had seen the Greek pointing his rifle at us. Perhaps, he added, he would not have shot at us but the risk wasn't worth taking. A recall had been the only option.

Would we really have been shot? It would have been utterly foolish to shoot women and children trying to evacuate the area in the presence of the UN, but this was war and in war anything is possible.

We had heard many horror stories during our stay in Cyprus. Among my memories is one of the time we were told that Greek soldiers had killed a woman and her children who were hiding in their bathroom. I recollect seeing pictures of this incident in newspapers.

Another terrible incident happened in my mother's village of Lefkoniko before the war started. A young Greek man who was troubled by mental illness, and whose behaviour was childlike at times, lived in the village. He had many Turkish friends and during the troubled times of which I'm writing he mixed with Turkish families while being told by activists that Greeks should not trade with, talk to or help Turks in any way.

EOKA activists discovered that he was continuing to befriend the Turkish community in the village. They captured him and hauled the poor man off to the church courtyard in the north part of the village. There they marched him to a tree, stretched his arms back around the trunk, nailed his hands in place and beat him senseless. One of the EOKA thugs cut off the man's penis and shoved it in his mouth. That poor, innocent child-man was left there for days, so that others who might have been thinking of helping Turks could see what would happen to them if they did.

The Green Line

Then there was the horrific story of Greek soldiers raping a pregnant Turkish woman before cutting her open and shooting her and her baby.

We heard about a Turkish civilian who had been shot in the neck with a machine gun and whose head was hanging off his neck by a piece of skin. I recall seeing a photo of this dreadful incident in a Turkish newspaper.

Are these just the kind of stories that inevitably circulate during times of war, or did they actually happen and get swept under the carpet? We heard of villagers being buried alive. I heard with my own ears people being burned alive. What fills man with such hatred that he does not hesitate to perform such acts?

I should add that, of course, horror stories of this kind were being told on both sides.

I heard about a group of Turkish Cypriot mujahits beating captured Greek soldiers with the butts of their rifles. One prisoner was beaten so badly that one of his eyes popped out of its socket. But a soldier from the Turkish mainland warned the mujahit who was guarding the prisoners that this constituted a war crime under international law and the mujahits would be in severe trouble. The soldier then left the scene, wanting nothing to do with the situation.

A mujahit asked a friend who was, like us, a tourist trapped by the hostilities, to shoot the prisoners as they were released one at a time from the house in which they were being kept. The man was horrified. "Sorry, I'm not a soldier and I've never killed anybody. I can't do that," he replied.

The mujahit was determined to find a way out of his predicament and avoid allegations of war crimes. "All right," he said, "you go in and set them free one at a time and I'll shoot them from behind. We can say they were shot trying to escape and nobody will know any better."

The tourist went into the house with a gun in his hand and looked, aghast, at the five beaten soldiers. Some had grotesquely broken limbs while others' skulls were smashed. He went over to the nearest prisoner and started to untie his hands. "You can go," he said quietly.

The prisoner was suspicious, not believing for a moment that he was really being freed. "Why?" he asked. "Someone will shoot me as soon as I start to run."

"I'm sorry, there's nothing more I can say or do," said the tourist. "This is a war, you are a soldier and this is what can happen to soldiers in a war. At least you have a chance to escape. Run as fast as you can."

He opened the door and nudged the prisoner, again urging him to run. The soldier burst out of the door, but he had not covered ten yards before he was cut down in a volley of shots. One by one the prisoners were released and one by one they ran to their deaths. Not one managed to escape.

To round off this collection of horror stories in suitably grim fashion, here is one that was told to new recruits doing their National Service in Northern Cyprus many years later.

The Green Line

During those bad times in 1974, the Greeks had taken over a village and the Turkish army was trying to take it back. A group of Greeks soldiers was positioned safely behind a building on the main road entering the village. The Turkish soldiers had engaged in a prolonged firefight with the Greeks, but were getting nowhere. A change of tactics was required.

The Turks began to run at the Greek position in threes and fours, putting down heavy fire as they advanced. But each time they ran forward they were cut down by fire from a machine gun. This carnage went on for some time until the Greeks decided to make a retreat, leaving their comrade with the machine gun to cover them. Again, Turkish soldiers tried to advance and again they were all gunned down.

The Turkish commander, deciding on another change of tactics, then ordered ten to fifteen of his men to advance at the same time – and it paid off. Eventually a couple of Turks reached the machine gunner's position, and he immediately raised his arms in surrender.

If he thought he would be taken prisoner and live to see his family again, he was mistaken. The Turkish commander, incensed and upset that he had lost so many of his men to this one combatant, cut off the Greek's arms and legs then left him on the road to die slowly in agonising pain.

"He had killed so many of the commander's men," the National Service sergeant told a silent, shocked audience. "He knew he would have to surrender eventually, yet he carried on slaughtering these young boys.

"You all know what it's like to be in a regiment; you get to know your comrades better than you know yourself. You will do anything to protect your mates. You're one big family. Seeing so many of your friends die like that will make you seek revenge, no question. Well, that commander got his revenge in the end, and who could blame him?"

CHAPTER THIRTEEN

Visiting a mysterious friend

The months had flown past us in a giddying whirlwind, and we had completely lost track of time. How long had we been in Cyprus? How long had we endured the fear and uncertainty of those troubles? Weeks? Months? What on earth, we wondered frantically, were our family and other loved ones going through back home, not knowing if they would ever see us again?

Mother booked us in to a small hotel in Nicosia. Here was yet another new experience for us, for we had never stayed in a hotel before. Not that our hotel debut was a wonderful or luxurious experience: the room was dark and dingy and the walls were covered in ancient white paint – or perhaps it was the colour of even more ancient plaster. The wooden floor was bare save for a red patterned rug in the middle of the room. The furnishings consisted of an old wooden table, two chairs and some single beds.

My brothers and I, excited nonetheless, ran into our new quarters and jumped on to the metal-framed beds, bickering about who was going to sleep where. It gradually dawned on us that there were four of us but only three beds.

"You two will have to share a bed," I told Erden and Niazy, taking charge of the situation, "'cos Mum will need to sleep on a bed."

"Wait here and be good," put in Mother. "I'm just going to go down and pay the man."

She shut the door and left us alone to explore our new living space. In fact, there wasn't much to do other than look out of the room's only window, but the view was nothing to write a postcard home about: another building directly opposite, which was blocking out most of the light.

We weren't impressed, but our interest suddenly perked up when we heard the sound of a man singing loudly from somewhere very near. We looked at each other and burst into giggles. The man's song went on and on, and before long the three of us had started to join in, imitating the strange sounds he was making. We were still singing and giggling when Mother rushed back into the room, closing the door quickly, shouting at us to stop and slapping each of us on the legs.

"What are you doing?" she cried "That's the imam from the mosque saying a prayer."

Well, we'd never heard anything like it before in our lives, short though they admittedly were. "We thought it was a man singing so we started to copy him," I replied, rubbing my leg ruefully.

Mother sighed. "I want you all to say after me: 'Bismillahir Rahmanir Rahim,'" she pronounced slowly, concluding with a brisk: "Then never do that again."

We did as she had told us and sat down quietly. We couldn't help thinking, though, that our little exercise in mimicry had been hysterically funny, and we exchanged smiling little glances.

Soon, Mother took us down to a small restaurant nearby to have some lunch. The restaurant had no frontage and was completely exposed to the outside world. The fixtures and fittings consisted of a few small tables with spindly, round, white metal legs and red Formica tops that were rimmed with plastic. Mother ordered some mixed liver and bread and the food soon arrived, accompanied by quartered lemons, parsley and a glass of water each.

I was ravenous and tucked in. "Hmm, this is really nice," I murmured appreciatively. And it was. The parsley and onions had been mixed into the liver and lemon had been squeezed into it. We dipped pieces of the delicious fresh bread into the juice, which we found was just as satisfying as munching the meat. We had found something we adored – so much so that we insisted on the same meal for the next few days and ate it with undisguised delight.

I doubt that we would have been quite so enthusiastic if we had known what the dish actually consisted of. Many years later, we were told that what we had devoured so keenly was a mixture of lamb's liver, lungs, heart, kidneys and oesophagus.

A few days after we had checked into the hotel, we made our way across Nicosia to a big white building. As we walked in and wandered along the corridors, it dawned on us boys that we were in a hospital. Mystified, I asked Mother: "What are we doing here, Mum?"

Her reply was short and not very helpful: "We've just come to visit a friend."

Before I could pose any further questions, a man in white overalls grabbed me by the hand and led me to into a nearby room. What on earth was going on?

I looked over at Mum, who had a certain guilty look about her but assured me all would be fine.

I grew ever more puzzled as two nurses in white uniforms removed my clothes and dressed me in a white hospital gown. They put me on an operating table and told me not to worry; it would all be over very soon.

But what would be over soon? What was happening? Why hadn't Mother said anything? This seemed a funny way of going about visiting a friend.

The real reason for our hospital visit was set before me. "Sünnet olacaksın (you are going to be circumcised)," explained one of the nurses, pinning my shoulder down. But I was none the wiser. Sünnet? What did that mean? Even if she had told me in English what was about to happen, I still wouldn't have had a clue.

"Don't worry, you'll be fine. Be a brave Turkish boy," said the other nurse comfortingly, stroking my cheek.

My puzzlement suddenly turned to raw pain as a surgeon appeared, yet another nurse held my feet down and the surgeon began sawing away at my manhood with a scalpel. "Good boy, you're so brave," came the soothing voice of the nurse. "It's nearly finished." I gritted my teeth and tensed all of my muscles, arching my back and fighting the pain, until the surgeon had completed his delicate task.

I then remembered all the times that I'd been told by my older brothers in England, and by our cousin Mustafa the practical joker, that we boys were holidaying in Cyprus mainly to have our willies chopped. I'd dismissed these as distasteful jokes and hadn't for a minute taken any of their comments seriously.

How could Mum not have told us what we were about to undergo? I felt betrayed, but I realised deep inside that if she had told us the truth about our visit to the hospital we would have been running from her like three headless chickens.

It was finished. "Well done," said a nurse. "We just have to bandage you up and then you can see your mother." They wheeled me out into the corridor, where Mother was waiting with her cousin Hasan.

"All done," said a nurse. "We didn't use anaesthetic because of the shortages, and he didn't even cry."

"Well done, Küfi," said Mother, leaning over to kiss me on the cheek. "Maşallah." That meant she was approving of my good, brave behaviour.

"You're a very brave boy," added Hasan.

Too right I was a brave boy. I'd just had my foreskin cut off without warning – and without anaesthetic.

I looked around for Niazy and Erden, eager to share my experience with my brothers. They wouldn't believe what had happened to me, I felt sure.

"Where are they?" I asked.

"They're in the room opposite having the same done," replied Mother calmly. "They should be out soon."

The door opened and Niazy and Erden were wheeled out, screaming their heads off in brotherly harmony.

"Ah, the poor boys didn't get any anaesthetic either," remarked Hasan.

But they had. "Yes, they were both put to sleep," confirmed a nurse. "They've only just woken up."

Mother began to calm the two wailing brothers down, giving them bags of sweets and a toy to play with. Her ruse worked and they grew as silent as church mice.

Hasan was curious. "Why were you crying?" he asked Niazy. "You couldn't have felt anything, yet Küfi was wide awake and he didn't cry."

"They must have been in shock when they woke up," suggested Mother.

Well, I can tell you the only reason I didn't cry was because I was still trying to figure out what on earth was happening to me. And before I could work it all out it was all over, so there was no point in crying.

The nurses placed the three of us in one bed in one of the hospital rooms, with Niazy and Erden at one end and I at the other. There was another bed in the room, and its inhabitant was a pretty young woman who had lost all her skin, from head to toe. The poor woman had been caught in a fire during the war and was undergoing painful daily treatment.

We stayed in hospital that night and I recall the nurses changing the woman's bandages on a regular basis. She would be crying in pain as they removed the last layer, which was always stuck to her raw flesh. But when the ordeal was over she would look over at us, smile and say nice things to us.

We left the hospital the next day and went to have a photo taken at a local photographer's studio. My nan had come to see us and gave us presents. We stood next to each other in our white gowns (which we had to wear for several days, as we were unable to wear underpants or trousers due to the circumcision), Maşallah hats, white socks and dirty old shoes, while the photographer snapped away. Every time we see these photos nowadays we crease up in laughter.

We made our way back to the village of İpsillat and spent some time with our grandparents, playing with our cousin and drinking pop at the coffee bar. But we had problems sleeping at night because there was still some pain from our circumcisions. We also had trouble urinating because of a scab that continually formed, blocking the passage.

Mother would take us out into the garden late at night and encourage us to go. We were almost bursting but it seemed no amount of straining would open the floodgates – then, suddenly, the blockage would open up and we would pee copiously, with enormous relief. We found great delight in the height and distance we were then able to pee, and we would hold competitions to find the champion urinator.

A few more days passed. One fine day Mother and her sister took us to the seaside. Hastily, we took off our gowns and ran over the hot sand into the sea, naked except for our bandaged willies. The sea was clear and warm and we enjoyed playing in the water. What's more, Mother thought that it would do us some good: the seawater would help heal our wounds.

We had been in the water for about half an hour when Niazy's attention was drawn to something untoward in my nether regions.

"Küfi, look!" he shouted, pointing a trembling finger at my bandaged parts. "Your willy has fallen off!"

"Oh no!" Erden was screaming and running back to tell mother what had happened.

I looked down, and was shocked at what I could not see. How could that have happened? "I can't believe it!" I cried.

"Can you feel anything at all?" Niazy asked in a sympathetic tone. "No, I can't feel a thing," I wailed. We started to walk back on to the beach where, to my amazement, Mother was laughing.

"Come here," she giggled. How could she laugh at a time like that?

"See, see, it's gone!" screamed Erden, compassion for my plight gleaming in his eyes.

I stood by mother as she began to unwrap the bandages to investigate. I couldn't bear to look and my eyes were firmly shut.

"Look silly boy, it's still there," said Mother, trying hard to suppress her laughter. "It's just shrivelled in the water. Looks like you won't need bandages any more."

I looked down to confirm her diagnosis, and gave thanks to God that I hadn't, after all, lost any of my important bits. Mother removed the bandages from both Niazy and Erden, and we all returned to the sea, bandage- and worry-free. The best thing of all was that we would no longer have to wear those silly, sissy white gowns.

CHAPTER FOURTEEN

Return home to another war

Eventually, the day dawned when we really were to leave. Our two-week holiday had lasted three months. We'd heard that Ozzy and his mother had left for England a couple of weeks before with the help of the British government. One sunny day, we bade farewell to Granddad and Nan, but not before Nan had pressed something into Mum's hands – some of her life savings, which she had stitched up inside a pillow, to help us on our journey back to London.

We made our way to Famagusta and took a ship to Mersin in Turkey. We found some seats together inside and sat for a while, chatting and playing. Then we ventured out on deck, to find a crowd of people who were pointing out to sea, chattering and laughing.

We had to find out the reason for their happiness, and scrambled to the front of the ship to see what all the fuss was about. We were greeted by the wonderful sight of five dolphins diving in and out of the water in front of the ship, just as if they were showing the skipper the way to Turkey. That certainly put a big smile on everyone's face.

On arrival at Mersin, we checked into a hotel for a night then took a coach to the Turkish capital, Ankara, followed by a train to Istanbul. That was one long, tiring journey, but Istanbul was nice and we stayed there for a few nights.

We did some sightseeing in Istanbul, taking in the historic, seventeenth century Blue Mosque, the extraordinary underground bazaar, the floating bridge that spans the Golden Horn and links Asia to Europe, and several other sights. Coming from the peace of İpsillat, it was mind-boggling to see how busy Istanbul life was: thousands of people rushing hither and thither, people carrying enormous loads on their backs to trade at the markets. This was a completely different world to the ones we knew.

But it wasn't long before we were on the plane that was to carry us back to London, and we were almost overcome with excitement at the thought of seeing our father and other brothers and sisters.

At Heathrow we collected our luggage and made our way through customs and out of the airport, to be met by a familiar, wet West London day. The air was cool and fresh compared to the heat of Cyprus, and it felt so good to be back in familiar surroundings. We piled into another familiar thing – a black taxi – and in no time were drawing up outside my father's fish and chip shop in Tooting Broadway.

There was no stopping us kids. We hurtled into the shop to come face to face with our amazed father. He'd had no idea whether we were dead or alive. The poor man could not quite believe what was happening. He grabbed and hugged us all, tears coursing down his face, and my sisters, who had been working with him in the shop, joined in the greetings and tears.

Emotional homecoming over, we all sat down and had a long, long chat before having something to eat. We had a lot to tell. At one point, I pulled a bullet out of my suitcase to show Father.

He examined the trophy. "This is a live bullet," he declared. "It could still explode. Let me look after it for you."

"No, it's OK Dad," I insisted. "Give it to me and I'll make it safe – I'll take the gunpowder out of the cartridge."

Dad was not convinced. "No, it's dangerous," he repeated.

But I was determined that he should give the bullet back to me and that I would show him how to make it safe. Reluctantly, he handed the disputed object over and followed me into the kitchen area.

"Look," I said, confidently putting the tip of the bullet up into the mouth of the tap in the kitchen sink then pulling the cartridge towards me, which forced the bullet out.

"Shall I empty the gunpowder into the sink, Dad?"

"Yes, empty it into the sink and run the cold water," he replied, chuckling and pinching me on the cheek, delighted at how savvy I had become.

It was indescribably great to be back home again, but we soon found that we had left one war behind only to enter another. Mother and Father never made up.

Father had warned Mother that we should not go to Cyprus because of the troubles that were brewing out there, but Mother had flaunted him and taken us boys out into what turned out to be a war zone. This new battle flared up the day we got back. Mother and Father argued constantly and did their best to keep out of each other's way until life was no longer bearable. This war lasted for about a year and ended with the pair of them breaking up and going their separate ways.

But we three boys had been hardened. We could take anything unexpected that life could throw at us. We had survived a war. We had seen and heard Man at his worst at an early age. What could possibly be worse than teetering on the edge of death? We were happy to have survived, we were glad to be alive and we were utterly determined to enjoy life to its fullest.

Time has shown that we three boys have been quite successful in life by taking risks in business ventures, getting up and starting again with each and every failure. Could this be because of what we've been through, or were we just three very, very lucky boys?

EPILOGUE

What follows is my opinion.

I am neither a politician nor a historian, but I do remember the stories told by my father of the Cyprus that was once united. He spoke of different ethnic groups of different faiths living side by side, working together, celebrating together, learning each other's languages. Recalling those tales, I feel it's a terrible shame that I may never be able to experience a united island, with Greeks and Turks living together without boundaries.

Arguments over who owns what in North and South continue to throw up an impenetrable barrier when it comes to attempted negotiations aimed at reunification of the island.

This island paradise has spent more than half a century in bitter turmoil. Is it not time to say enough is enough? Why can we not achieve once again what our grandfathers and great-grandfathers did, and live together in harmony?

My heart goes out to all those that have suffered: Turkish, Greek, Greek Cypriot, Turkish Cypriot and British, and all those who have lost loved ones. I believe

The Green Line

it is time for the past to be put to rest once and for all and to start building bridges that will last for ever.

One cannot change the past, but one can change the future.